Thoughtfully and patiently, *Seeking Spirit* by Linda Trinh .... tion of how the search for belonging can create a heightened awareness of and longing for a spiritual life. Through the story of her own family, Trinh traces the threads that bind her to her ancestors, showing us all how faith and peace don't begin with answers, but with learning to live with the questions."

— **Hollay Ghadery**, award-winning author of *Fuse*

This rich spiritual memoir of inner seeking by Linda Trinh is an account well worth reading. In it, she reveals much, crafting in words, her experience of the ineffable journey the soul takes through her life. Her spiritual touchstones are multiple and reflect the worlds of her Vietnamese family and upbringing as well as the cultures of the books she read in her childhood and growing up in Winnipeg. I work to make the mundane spiritual, she says at one point, and this I believe is the task of all of us for living our lives with meaning, purpose and vitality.

— **Sally Ito**, author of *Emperor's Orphans*

Seeking Spirit by Linda Trinh is a well-written, beautiful book. It portrays her experience in search of the divine feminine. Trinh's spiritual journey commences as she realizes with all that she has, still something is missing. And so, begins a profound and intimate spiritual journey in search of the sacred. Incorporating hybridity of form, lyricism, and emotional honesty, I highly recommend this book. Seeking Spirit deeply resonated with me and is a book that I will come back to again and again.

— **Rowan McCandless**, author of *Persephone's Children; A Life in Fragments* and Governor Generals nonfiction finalist

Linda Trinh's memoir *Seeking Spirit* is an honest, vulnerable, and tenderly crafted account of how she navigates her spirituality against a backdrop of brutal losses, grief, and setbacks. She draws us close as she exposes the complexities of believing, displaying an acute desire to know what is not known. As a fellow Vietnamese-Canadian who grew up spiritually untethered, this book made me feel seen in ways I never knew I needed.

— **Mai Nguyen**, author of *Sunshine Nails*

For anyone who has ever sought spiritual connection or cultural belonging, Linda Trinh's narrative reads as both deeply personal and strikingly familiar. *Seeking Spirit* is more than just a memoir, however; it is an offering to the sacred deities of motherhood and the divine spirits of writing.

— **Shanon Sinn**, author of *The Haunting of Vancouver Island*

An intriguing and stunning tale of a Vietnamese Canadian woman who seeks more to her successful immigrant life as a wife and mother thriving in Winnipeg. Trinh asks substantive questions and offers rich and astonishing insights in her inventive memoir of spirituality and international travel. What does it mean to find oneself through the meticulous excavation of family, culture, and motherhood? What does it mean to feel alienated and unfulfilled and also survive deep personal loss? How does someone carry their ancestors with them from childhood? Trinh enlightens, provokes, and meditatively reflects.

—**Lindsay Wong**, author of *The Woo-Woo*
and *Tell Me Pleasant Things about Immortality*

SEEKING
SPIRIT

A Vietnamese
(Non)Buddhist
Memoir

MIROLAND IMPRINT 48

Canadä

ONTARIO ARTS COUNCIL
CONSEIL DES ARTS DE L'ONTARIO

an Ontario government agency
un organisme du gouvernement de l'Ontario

Ontario

Canada Council   Conseil des arts
for the Arts   du Canada

Guernica Editions Inc. acknowledges the support of
the Canada Council for the Arts and the Ontario Arts Council.
The Ontario Arts Council is an agency of the Government of Ontario.

We acknowledge the financial support of the Government of Canada.

Linda Trinh

SEEKING SPIRIT

A Vietnamese (Non)Buddhist Memoir

MiroLand
publishers
TORONTO • CHICAGO
BUFFALO • LANCASTER (U.K.)
2025

Guernica Founder: Antonio D'Alfonso

Michael Mirolla, general editor
Julie Roorda, editor
Cover design and interior design: Rafael Chimicatti
Cover images: Lewis J Goetz and Adrian Pelletier/Unsplash

Guernica Editions Inc.
1241 Marble Rock Rd., Gananoque, ON K7G 2V4
2250 Military Road, Tonawanda, N.Y. 14150-6000 U.S.A.
www.guernicaeditions.com

Distributors:
Independent Publishers Group (IPG)
600 North Pulaski Road, Chicago IL 60624
University of Toronto Press Distribution (UTP)
5201 Dufferin Street, Toronto (ON), Canada M3H 5T8

First edition.
Printed in Canada.

Legal Deposit—First Quarter
Library of Congress Catalog Card Number: 2024945786
Library and Archives Canada Cataloguing in Publication
Title: Seeking spirit : a Vietnamese (non)Buddhist memoir / Linda Trinh.
Names: Trinh, Linda, author.
Description: "MiroLand imprint 48." | Includes index.
Identifiers: Canadiana (print) 20240460677 | Canadiana (ebook) 20240462467
ISBN 9781771839549 (softcover) | ISBN 9781771839556 (EPUB)
Subjects: LCSH: Trinh, Linda. | LCSH: Trinh, Linda—Religion.
LCSH: Spirituality. | CSH: Authors, Canadian (English)—21st century—
Biography. CSH: Vietnamese Canadians—Biography.
LCGFT: Autobiographies.
Classification: LCC PS8639.R575 Z46 2025 | DDC C814/.6—dc23

For all seekers

Contents

Foreword

LINDA TRINH WAS NEW TO ME when I learned that she was writing spiritual memoir. That was in 2020, in a master class about a genre that was—still is—an outlier in the Canadian literary landscape. (And a shout-out here to the CNFC [Canadian Nonfiction Collective] for hosting.) What I did not know then that I know now is that Linda is at the forefront of a wave of gifted writers who are reclaiming the genre, re-framing how we speak about the human journey.

Spiritual life writing can take the shape of biography, autobiography, memoir, ethnography, poetry, and so on. You don't have to know the forms to appreciate their power. Classics, such as the (three-volume) *Life* of the Spanish Counter-Reformation genius, Teresa of Avila, remain a cornerstone in the western literary canon, thanks to the fact that the genre dates to the fourth century and another rabble rouser, Augustine of Hippo. Incidentally, his *Confessions* is an Amazon bestseller.

But maybe you're a fan of memoirs by Joy Harjo, Helen Knott, Anne Lamott, or Dani Shapiro. You love Eve Joseph's award-winning *In the Slender Margin*, or *Between Gods* by Alison Pick. Maybe you've been gifted the arresting poetry of Betsy Warland or Hollay Ghadery's genre-busting books. Musicians of an age likely own well-thumbed copies of *Rumours of Glory* by the iconic Bruce Cockburn. If any such works are on your radar, then you're aware of spiritual life writing (and maybe didn't know it). The trouble isn't with the genre, or the power of its reach. The trouble is that spirituality has a branding problem. *Seeking Spirit* will change that, I expect, in which case we'll see a flowering of the critical reception these beloved works deserve.

Literary treatments of well, everything, are hallmarks of an open, plu-ralistic society. We already welcome multi-generational, globally inflected stories that speak to the living of the dead. It's time to celebrate the ta-boo-breakers, writers who risk complicating notions of spirit, seeking, faith, religion, ritual, and ceremony as part of simply speaking openly about their lives and family histories. Watch how this spiritual memoir—and make no mistake, that's what Linda Trinh has written—will do what her kids books do for families and libraries and schools throughout North America.

Open doors.

Enlighten minds.

Inspire conversations.

So, congratulations. You hold in your hands a title in which a woman's quest for meaning is told without apology or hedging. *Seeking Spirit* is a beautifully wrought exploration of territory that fiction writer and scholar Linda Sexson called "ordinarily sacred." Sexson's (1982) contention that "improvising may be the religious ritual and thought of the contemporary world" has an urgency now that speaks directly to the growing need for authenticity, representation, and for new life breathed into ancient forms. At long last, *Seeking Spirit* marks a threshold in Canadian publishing, as writers and poets with mixed identities and orientations—many of them having laboured in the margins—take the lead in plumbing the fullness of human experience unapologetically, joyously, critically, empathetically. May these works be greeted with the generosity of spirit they deserve.

Treaty One territory is home to Linda Trinh and her family. Raised in Winnipeg, the daughter of Vietnamese immigrants, here is a writer with a calling. World-bridging is the beating heart of her storytelling instincts. Here is work that reckons lovingly with loss and absence across geographies as across the generations, that traces that search for the ineffable, the urge to mythologize, ritualize, to map the soul's desires. Here is work grounded in a mindful (some would say Buddhist) quiet, twinned with a (some would say prairie) sense of freedom and deep love of community. *Seeking Spirit* is her first memoir, but make no mistake, it is classic Trinh—drawing us close, in an intimate voice, in a space of gentleness and care, in essay after essay that is shot through with wonder. Watch what happens when you close the book and fall back into ordinary time, staring at that rat's nest of lowly tasks and unanswered emails. Is a part of you still dreaming? Do you feel your body shifting, a bone-deep gratitude taking hold? Maybe what you're feeling is permission, finally, to breathe.

Susan Scott
Editor, *Body & Soul: Stories for Skeptics and Seekers*
Waterloo, Ontario
July 2024

Prologue

Is this it?

I had asked myself that question many times since reaching adulthood. Living on the surface of my life felt like a superficial existence, and by not mining deeper to the mantle, outer core and inner core, I had not fully unearthed its richness and depth. As I peered beyond the horizon to the rest of my life, endless blue sky and glittering snow on the prairies where I made my home, I foresaw more of the same—an infinite stretch of ordinary life. The routine consisted of waking up and going to work, fixing the same meals, lamenting over the fast-paced nature of the daily grind, then wishing for just a moment to be able to take a full breath.

I had everything I thought I should want. I was living out the typical immigrant's dream, to be a wife and a mother, someone who worked a steady job and owned a house in the suburbs. And yet, the questions still bubbled up.

Is this it? What is missing?

I was blessed with love, family, and valuable experiences, and yet, my gratefulness never lasted long. My feelings dissipated into the ether, the empty space between the stars, a dark void, a nothingness found throughout the universe. I felt this empty space deep within myself not filled with anything I could touch, taste, or possess, no matter how hard I tried. Even when I was content in the other areas of my life, this part of myself still felt empty.

This empty space called out for spirit.

When I thought about "spirit," I imagined some sort of light that illuminated outside and inside. I imagined an awakening, an enlightenment of body, mind, and soul that connected me to something that transcended the ordinariness of life.

I believed spirituality could exist within the realm of institutional religion and also without any religious foundation. Prayers, rituals, and ceremonies have long been performed and practised by us all, through generations past, in all parts of the world.

Swirling around me were the spirits of my ancestors from Vietnam, the country of my birth, the Buddhist traditions of my childhood, as well as the goddesses and gods of the mythologies of long-ago civilizations. From all these bits and pieces of myself, I felt the need to fashion a mantle to ward off the prairie chill. I longed to invite spirit in, and to sense its spark within myself.

How do I find what I am seeking?

In my darkest fantasies or perhaps my lightest moments, I wondered what it would be like to leave it all behind and create a different life in a different way in a different space. Quit my job. Travel the world. Find myself. What would it be like to leave all my loved ones and all my responsibilities? That might be too extreme. I didn't want to leave behind the life that I had built. I was not trying to escape my life, only to enrich it.

There had to be another way. A middle path. I needed to seek spirit within the structure of my own life.

I doubt I am the only one who has felt this empty space. I can't imagine I am alone in my need for something more.

This is my journey through ice and fire, space and time, walking along the edges of the land of the living and the land beyond, believing and questioning, stumbling and soaring. This is my path of what I learned and what I had to unlearn to seek the sacred. My journey is only one of many paths that a seeker may take. Perhaps by weaving the pattern of my path, a familiar thread or recognizable fabric might emerge that shows how we are all interconnected.

This interconnection exists between the stars as well. While I see nothing-ness in space, space is truly not empty; instead, it is filled with interstellar gas and dust. The dust of the stars gave life to me and to all life in the universe. The starlight burns brilliantly in the darkness. Perhaps, like space, I am not empty, perhaps I am not nothingness. I need to seek to find my own interconnection between the stars.

PART I
SPIRIT STUDIED

One: Incense and Ancestors

GROWING UP, it WAS my job to clean Ba's altar every month, sweeping away dust, sweeping away grey ashes from the incense holder, sweeping away last month's prayers and wishes. My dad peered through his black and white photo behind glass while I worked. Standing on a kitchen chair so I could reach the altar on top of the wall unit, I dusted the two plastic candles, red candles, each topped with a red light bulb to simulate candlelight. The two stood guard on either side of his framed photo. I wiped down the red and gold incense holder in front of his picture, maneuvering around the spot where the real incense went and around the three joss sticks made of plastic, each complete with a miniscule glowing bulb. I always tried to clean the black singe mark on the middle plastic joss stick, never surprised that month after month the stain remained.

I was seven when he died. I woke up to Má lying beside me and Jen. "Ba mất" was all my mom said. Dad's lost. She cried into my shoulder, short bursts of sound dampened by silence. She swallowed her grief as it began to bubble up inside her, trying to stop it before it got away from her. I imagined her fists were clenched in the darkness. Her tears were wet on my pyjamas and I shivered. Jen was turned away from us on the bed, her form shaking on the well-worn mattress. I don't remember crying. I must have. The bed was hot and cramped, yet I felt as if I was encased in ice, apart from them. I would have liked more words from Má, words to comfort my little child mind, words to help me, words to make it bearable. I had never visited him in the hospital. And I never said goodbye.

Má made offerings to Ba and to all the ancestors. On death anniversaries and at Tết, the Lunar New Year, and every new moon, she cúnged with flowers and food. There was fruit, if nothing else. She made offerings to our loved ones who had passed beyond the land of the living. Má lit incense in front of Ba's altar. My mom's palms pressed a fragrant joss stick between them in front of her heart. With prayers on her lips and eyes focussed, she peered through the earthly objects into the spirit world. She bowed her head three times.

Cúng happened once a month, at a specific time, but I didn't know much about the cycles of the moon growing up. I'd be nervous searching through the fridge for fruit to eat. "Má, have the apples been cúnged?"

"No, don't touch them!" she'd yell in Vietnamese.

I'd shut the door quickly and jump away from the fridge. I didn't mean to touch them. Eating un-cúnged fruit felt like the ultimate sin, like I was stealing out of the ancestors' own mouths.

On cúng days, Má scurried around the kitchen before the sun came up, slamming drawers and clinking dishes with extra vigour to ensure her daughters dared not sleep in. She was the chef and house manager and I was the server and dishwasher. Three place settings at Ba's altar. Three place settings at the dinner table. Five place settings at the coffee table. Who these place settings were for was something I didn't know. I laid out a bowl of rice, chopsticks, tea and Coke, small bowls of fish sauce or soya sauce, some with chilli and some without, at each place setting. I set out platters of fresh apples and oranges and other fruit in season. The menu would change. It could be vegetarian or meat-friendly—egg rolls, fish maw soup, chicken curry, stir fried noodles -- and dessert of layered gelatin or cassava cake would sometimes be served. Tomatoes stuffed with tofu, and rice paper wraps were my favourites. I brought the food from the kitchen and did my arrangement. When Má came to do her final inspection, she always rearranged what I did. No, the curry should be next to the fish, the fruit should be at the head of the table.

Once she was sure the ancestors would be pleased, she lit the joss sticks and said her prayers. We were only allowed to eat after the incense burned away completely. I sat in the kitchen wondering—was the incense an invitation to the meal? Was that how our family knew to stop their wanderings and come to our house? Or were they always with us and the incense was the vehicle through which they could consume the offerings? Did kids who grew up in Filipino or Indigenous or Ukrainian homes in Winnipeg have questions about their rituals?

Watching Má in front of my dad's altar, we were both around the same height, 5'2" and had slim builds but never considered ourselves thin. Má wore glasses that left bruises on the sensitive skin on the bridge of her nose. She kept her black permed hair in a neat short bob and friends would comment her pale skin appeared bright. My skin had a darker colouring, taking after Ba; I usually wore my straight black hair past my shoulders, and my face was round as a clock, as one of my aunts used to say.

I imagined her the morning after he passed away, ready to tell Jen and me when we woke up. I imagined her eyes dry, shock taking over, no tears flowing. What did Ba promise my mom to make her move away from her family in Vietnam, away from the life she knew, to cross an ocean to a land of an uncertain future? Ba was the adventurous one according to Jen; I wouldn't know. He was the dreamer, the one yearning for a different life, comfortable with the risks and rewards. Má wanted peace, to be encircled by family and friends, to live a simple life. And now Ba had left her alone, in a country not her own, with his brothers and sisters, not hers. Halfway around the world, Má's own mom and her sisters were so far away. We were all supposed to be together, we were supposed to become prosperous: Ba a successful businessman, Má a supportive wife, and two well-behaved educated daughters who would grow up to be doctors. A house in the suburbs with a well-manicured lawn. Two cars in the double garage. Dinner parties with friends. This was the immigrant dream.

The weight of Má's disappointment tied itself around her shoulders and pulled them down as she bent over her sewing machine day after day. She could not have imagined this was how her life would turn out—living in an 800-square foot one-storey house in wintery Winnipeg where we extended the fold-out couch every night in the living room. That was her bedroom. She sacrificed her own space so each of us had our own tiny room that fit a twin bed and a hand-me-down dresser.

I would open every window and fling wide the front door, yet the incense clung to us, the air smoggy. Grey ash collected under the burning joss sticks. On every inhale, I tasted the smoke at the back of my throat, bitter yet fragrant, as if swallowing a charred rose petal. I studied the shapes and images in the dancing incense smoke, sometimes circles or waves, but sometimes a galloping horse with slim legs and a thick tail. I smiled. Ba had been born in the year of the Horse.

Má never sat me down and to tell me this was how we pray, this was why we pray, this was why we make offerings to the ancestors. A frequent theme during my childhood: she didn't owe me, her daughter, an explanation. She did what she did and expected me to obey. I wondered if other kids asked questions. Mommy, why do we have a Christmas tree? What's heaven? Why do we go to Synagogue? How does God hear our prayers? Were there other kids like me, rooted in the rituals of the belief system into which they were born, yet questioning?

She would pass an incense stick to me, the tip a ring of red embers, grey smoke curling up to the ceiling. My turn to pray? My throat tightened, and my skin became slick with panic. I mimicked as best I dared. The ancestors must have known I was a fake.

Growing up. I was bits and pieces of raw materials. Was there enough fabric to stitch together a coherent ensemble of myself? Was it possible the pieces could come together at all with their frayed and jagged edges? There were no binding elements, the threads, the things in between the spaces, that connected one to another and to another. I wasn't put together yet.

I pieced together what I could. There is a connection to those who have passed beyond this life, a connection that transcends death. Cúng is the ritual through which we connect with the spirit world; by making offerings, we symbolically share a meal with those who are no longer with us. In doing so, they remain with us. Perhaps the incense smoke opens the gateway between the visible and the unseen, where spirits know each other without form. The spirit world does not belong in a house of worship. Spirits live alongside us, waiting to be invited into our houses, to be called to our sides. Ancestor worship existed before institutional religions emerged in Vietnam. Buddhism enveloped, Christianity encircled, Cao Đài encased, yet ancestor worship remained. This is what I grew up knowing. Knowing is not the same as believing.

When we left Vietnam as a family of four, I was three and Jen was ten. My parents had lived through the American War in Vietnam and crossed the ocean for new opportunities abroad. After only a few years in Canada, Ba passed away, sixteen days before he could fulfill his dream of becoming a Canadian citizen. Then we were three. After Ba passed away, we lived in a one-bedroom apartment, then a two-storey green-trimmed house, then a third-floor apartment, then a tiny house where Má slept on the fold-out couch, all within a few blocks between Notre Dame and Sargent, Beverley and Simcoe in the West End of Winnipeg. My mom, my sister, and I co-cooned ourselves within the world we knew.

Houses were packed close together and garages were tagged with gang graffiti. Overgrown grass and weeds in the front yards, and beer cans and broken glass along the sidewalk were not an unusual sight. Police sirens blaring at all hours was not uncommon. Neighbours were immigrants like us, or first-generation Canadians. We were all brushing up against each others' realities. In some ways, we were alike, all stumbling toward what it meant to be defined as Canadian. We were all exposed to Thanksgiving dinners and Easter egg hunts, blizzards and wind chill factors.

Má told me to come home from school right away and start my home-work. After I turned the deadbolt, I found things to amuse myself—playing imaginary games with blonde Barbies, creating lives and stories of my own, acting out scenes of mythology and fairy tales was how I passed the time. Glancing out the window, I saw my classmates walk by with Slurpees in their hands and laughing, playing badminton in the street, and lining up for the ice cream guy when he rang his bell riding by. I didn't line up for ice cream. I didn't play in the street. I stayed inside. I felt okay about this, remembering that I did have kids to hang out with on the playground. I wasn't *that girl* who roamed the outer grassy field alone until the bell rang, I was *that girl* who trailed behind the girls with shiny hair and sparkly smiles—who no one talked to directly.

In so many ways, I was not like the other kids in my school, who were mostly from Portuguese, Filipino and Indigenous backgrounds. Kids talked about seeing each other at Sunday school and communion prepara-tions. Kids talked about what their moms and dads did with them on the weekends. What church do you go to? What do you do with your mom and dad?

I don't go to church.

I don't have a dad.

I would have to explain my differences. So I said very little at all.

The world outside my front door was unfamiliar and the world inside was not wholly familiar. Heaven and God and Jesus outside and incense and ancestors and the Buddha inside.

Was I not enough of something—Canada where I landed? Or was I not enough of something else—Vietnam where I was born? The space between Canada and Vietnam, neither inside or outside those countries and those identities. The space in between. That's where I existed. I wanted to piece together the raw bits of myself. I knew I needed to wait, watch, and work to find the binding material to make myself whole. I was bits and pieces of raw material.

*　*　*

When I was in junior high, my sister volunteered at the Saigon Pavilion during Folklorama, a well-known multicultural festival in Winnipeg that highlights cultures and countries of the world. At community centres, high school gyms, and other venues, cultural societies and associations in the city invite others to step into their worlds.

Jen performed in the dance of the Trưng sisters. She played the role of Trưng Trắc and wore a red tunic and a golden headdress like a halo, signifying that she was carrying out the will of heaven. Her face was firm, eyes gazing beyond the audience, and her jaw set. During the first half of the dance, she stood on wooden steps behind an elephant built of timber and construction paper, one arm bent on her hip, the other arm wielding a sword pointed straight out in front of her. A fellow dancer, playing the role of Trưng Nhị, stood behind Jen on more wooden steps behind a second constructed elephant. The elephants were painted in shades of grey with ivory tusks and colourful ribbons down their backsides. This gave the audience the impression that Trưng Trắc and Trưng Nhị rode on the backs of these mighty beasts—war elephants, ready for battle.

Their soldiers wore yellow tunics with red sashes, and black boots, and held shiny metal swords. For this dance, the choreographer Cô Lý had instructed them not to smile. For other dances, she usually highlighted the opposite. Remember to smile during the fan dance. Smile during the drum dance. And smile during the umbrella dance. Those dances showcased femininity and gentleness through graceful steps, soft arms and long lines. Shuffle, shuffle, and turn. Swoop the arm across the chest and down to the floor. Bend back slowly. In contrast, the dance of the Trưng sisters had quick and controlled movements conveying strength and power. March, march, look right, look left, sword out, bend knees, brisk turn, thrust blade forward, and advance the line. These were not the movements of girls, but the movements of warriors. This was war, a battle to preserve Vietnamese identity.

Jen must have performed this dance more than a dozen times over the week. There were three shows a night, and the dance of the Trưng sisters was usually performed at each show; it was the Pavilion's most popular dance. It seemed like every Vietnamese person knew the tale. When the emcee described the upcoming dance, the Vietnamese people in the audience nodded their heads, "Of course of course, we know, get on with it."

Long ago and far away, in the land of my ancestors, the people of Vietnam prayed to be free. It was a tale told time and time again throughout the ages, both in the old world and in the new world—a distinct culture fighting for independence against a foreign power. The mighty Middle Kingdom of China had cast its shadow upon Vietnam in the first century B.C.E.

After two thousand years, the historical truth of the two sisters, Trưng Trắc and Trưng Nhị, has evaporated into the winds of time, carried along by gusts of myth throughout the centuries. In the most traditional account of events, the one most widely reported by historians, the Trưng sisters were born into a noble family, their father part of the Lạc lords living in the Red River Delta valley, in Giao Chỉ province. Presently, this is close to Hà Nội in northern Vietnam. The Lạc lords believed they were descendants of the Hùng kings as part of the origin story of the Vietnamese people. The mountain fairy Âu Cơ and the sea dragon Lạc Long Quân had one hundred children together. When they parted ways, fifty children went with their mother to the mountains where they became the highlanders. Fifty children went with their father to the seashore where they became the Hùng kings of the Lạc people.

Even after two hundred years of governance, the Lạc people had no love for their Chinese rulers of the Han Dynasty. In an act intended to secure obedience, the Chinese Administrator had Trưng Trắc's husband, Thi Sách, executed for insurrection. This act had the opposite effect. Trưng Trắc set aside her mourning clothes and took up sword and shield in 40 C.E.

The sisters raised a rebellion army of women and men and drove out the Chinese through quick and decisive raids and battles. Trưng Trắc was crowned queen and she ruled for three years. Yet in 43 C.E., the Chinese came back, and defeated the Trưng sisters.

The historical accounts do not mention the sisters riding elephants into battle. There are different accounts of their deaths. The account closest to the hearts of the Vietnamese is that the sisters drowned themselves in the Hát River, preserving their honour for eternity. Yet others have written they were captured, executed, and their heads delivered back to the Han capital.

The Trưng sisters had fallen.

And the legend of Hai Bà Trưng, two sisters Trưng, was born.

The first time I saw the dance of Hai Bà Trưng performed, tears welled up in my eyes and goose pimples dotted along the back of my neck and down my bare arms. The Duckworth Centre at the University of Winnipeg where the Pavilion was held was well air-conditioned during muggy August. Yet I felt heat rise to my cheeks and out through the top of my head. I crossed my arms over my chest to hold myself together, my reaction was so immediate.

Mighty warrior women. Mighty Vietnamese women. I felt this story deep in my bones, resonating through my blood. This was my introduction to the two sisters, my first glimpse into my own history. The Trưng sisters were certainly not part of the curriculum at General Wolfe School in the West End.

Growing up in Canada, I knew about European explorers and I knew about ancient Egypt. Yet I knew very little about the history of the country of my birth. I was three when we emigrated, and I had visited Vietnam only once before entering junior high. The Vietnam War, phở noodle soup, and people on motorbikes came quickest to mind when I thought about where I was born.

I focussed on Jen standing stationary on her war elephant. What was going through her mind? She had just deployed her army to battle the greater force of the Chinese. Was she fearful? Was she determined to see this to the end? When did Trưng Trắc know she was going to be defeated? When did she decide to give up her mortal life? Trưng Trắc, channelled through my sister, reached out from the past. Trưng Trắc illuminated my path through the mists of the spirit realm, highlighting the Vietnamese pull to the otherworldly.

Ever since the summer of the Saigon Pavilion, Trưng Trắc has been nearby. She became my role model; I was a shy girl who loved to read and play games of imagination, but I did not see myself in my cherished Lucy Maud Montgomery books and blonde Barbie dolls. It was the first time I saw myself, a Vietnamese girl, represented anywhere.

Trưng Trắc was a whisper in the wind after I closed the front door. She was a flash of light after I turned off the lamp in my bedroom. She was a heroine from the land of my ancestors. Powerful and proud. A thread wove its way from Trưng Trắc through the generations to me. She was not far, she was close.

I followed the thread that linked me to Trưng Trắc. Through her, I discovered the threads that bound me to my family, that bound me to my dad, in the realm of the spirits.

Ba had passed on before I celebrated my eighth birthday. He went into the hospital and never came out. I only recall flashes—wavy black hair and brown sunglasses, a belly laugh that was contagious and hands tanned like leather, wrinkled yet warm. Everyone said I'd inherited my darker skin from Ba, while Jen took after Má. My memories of him as bone and flesh are faded and fragmented.

And yet, after his passing, I saw him everyday staring through his photo from his altar. We shared meals together of rice, bi soup, pan fried pork, after Má cúnged. I saw him when I cleaned his altar every month. When I envision Ba, I see him in black and white as a young man in his mid-twenties from his altar photo. Even though I never knew that man in real life, the man from the picture has been a presence in my life.

The veil between the living and the dead is thin. Family passes on and yet they remain. My family swirls around me, ghosts without form yet true to essence. A hand at my back, a caress on my cheek. Whispering to me, steadying my feet. They are never far from this world. Not peering down from heaven but walking alongside me. Slipping in between the veil of human breath and shadow existence.

A crack in the window, a doorway not quite shut, a lid slightly ajar.

Enough of an opening through which

> light may pass,
> air may flow,
> water may seep,
> and spirit may come.

* * *

I was fully immersed in Vietnamese spiritual practice when I was twenty-five years old, out of university and working, and I travelled to Vietnam with Má and Jen. We went there to mark the end of the two-year mourning period for my Bà Ngoại, my maternal grandmother. Since landing in Canada for the first time on a snowy St. Valentine's Day at age three, this was my fourth trip back to Vietnam.

I was nine years old on our first trip back. Má had tears in her eyes as we walked off the plane. She was home. I, on the other hand, was visiting a foreign country. Everything was different from what I knew. I couldn't read the signage around me. The buildings were four or five storeys tall and jammed up against one another like building blocks. A sea of Hondas and bikes, never-ending waves of traffic merging and weaving together, flooded the streets. And the strangest part—there were Vietnamese people everywhere. Having grown up on the Canadian prairies, I felt culture shock. Also, I was a constant curiosity. Because of my mannerisms and clothing choices, people stared at me wherever I went. One person whispered "Việt Kiều." They all nodded. Ahhh … overseas Vietnamese. I was separate from them. Not enough of something. Again.

On this fourth trip back to Vietnam, two years to the day after Bà Ngoại's passing, the family gathered at her house for her đám giỗ, the ceremony to end the mourning period. Offerings had been made for Bà Ngoại for the first forty-nine days after her passing, then a ceremony was held after 100 days, then another ceremony was held after one year, then another ceremony after two years, or so says the internet search I did. Má did not offer up any explanations, just as it was throughout my childhood. She just said we were going and so we bought plane tickets.

A monk stood next to Bà Ngoại's altar in his saffron robes. His prayer beads clicked in his slick palms as droplets of sweat formed on his shiny head. Words popped from his mouth like soap bubbles. The monk spoke Buddha's name, my mom's name, my sister's name, my name. This was all the Vietnamese I deciphered from his tones. Maybe the rest was about blessings and teachings of the Buddha, words to comfort those left behind.

Má and Jen, my uncles and aunts, my cousins and I were all on the floor kneeling on reed mats, heads bowed, wrapped in white mourning clothes, facing the monk and the altar. My white headband was itchy against my forehead.

A red tablecloth covered the wooden altar, with yellow tassels that hung over the edges. Bà Ngoại, dignified and proper, looked on from the afterlife behind a pane of glass. In the photo, taken of her in her seventies, she wore her best áo dài, silvery mai flowers embroidered on cool grey silk. Her face was wrinkled, and her eyes were sharp, shining, observing everything. I saw my mom in my grandmother's expression. Red candles stood guard on either side of the photo and an incense burner sat in front. Offerings of hot tea and small plates of rice, chopped pork, fish soup, and fresh mangoes were laid out on the table.

Má cúnging at home in Canada provided me with an introduction to these rituals and to the idea of ancestor worship. Yet for all I knew growing up, she could have been making up these practices herself. Living and breathing the rituals here in Vietnam wove its own spell around me. It provided an anchor of legitimacy. I had not realized I craved that legitimacy.

The monk rang the bronze bell with a quick flick of his wrist, a signal for us to bow three times. I was not able to feel my legs underneath me as I kneeled. I lowered my head and body. A droplet of sweat slid off the end of my nose and fell on the reed mat. I tried to imitate my relatives, praying not to make a mistake or to stand out. Everyone here, except me and my mom and my sister, lived in Vietnam. But Má had grown up in this house. Jen had spent the first ten years of her life in this country. I was the only visitor here, the only foreigner.

The monk pointed to the incense burner with another quick motion of his hand and everyone stood up. I followed, not understanding what I was doing. I followed Má and Jen to the altar. I was outside my comfort, outside my reality, outside myself. My mom handed me three joss sticks already lit, the rings of red ember smouldering to ash. Clasping the incense sticks in front of me, I bowed three times just like the others did. Wisps of incense swirled to heaven, to the afterlife.

I focussed my mind on my Bà Ngoại. I did not want Bà Ngoại to see me as a fake.

I slipped away from myself. I imagined myself entwining with the soft sounds of the monk's chant and rose into the empty spaces above the altar. I imagined being lost behind the veil in the realm of ancestors. I was chasing after a shadow, trying to catch up to it, to grasp it. Mist and fog blurred my sight.

Have you seen my Bà Ngoại? I've lost her. I've lost her.

I soared, searching. I believed I could see her in front of me. Yet as hard as I tried, I could not close the distance between us.

***

Two years before, when I was twenty-three, Bà Ngoại had passed away suddenly. She had not been suffering from any serious ailments. There was a knock at the door when we were all asleep, full darkness outside. Two of my cousins had the burden of relaying the news, their eyes downcast as they crossed the threshold. They had received the call from Vietnam; no one called us directly as this news needed to be conveyed in-person. Bà Ngoại was not their grandmother, as my cousins in Canada were related through my dad. Má wailed and sobbed, bent over as she sat on her bed-couch, my arm threaded through her arm, my cousin's arm on her back, arms entangling and overlapping.

This was spontaneous sorrow, a rupture of the heart, violent and quick. Má made sounds deep in her throat I had never heard before, a low-pitched tone trying to suck in enough air. I wondered if this had been her immediate reaction all those years ago to losing Ba, before she had to swallow it all down to tell Jen and me the news. I wondered what kind of relationship she and Bà Ngoại had had. How had Má felt leaving her mom to come to Canada? Had Bà Ngoại passed on ancestor worship to Má, teaching her how to cúng and light incense? Had Bà Ngoại explained what the incense meant? Had Bà Ngoại explained why?

Má was on a plane to Vietnam by herself a few days later, grief her only travelling companion. We did not go with her this time. As I hugged her at the airport, my mom's eyes were no longer on us, her daughters, but gazing across the ocean, to the house where she had grown up in Trảng Bàng, to the house where she would gather with her siblings to lay their mother to rest.

I was again in between spaces in my experience of grief. With my dad, I didn't know of anyone else who had lost a parent at a young age. All my cousins had their moms and dads. With my Bà Ngoại, I didn't know of anyone else who had lost a grandparent who lived so far away. Jen and I went home to an empty house and continued our normal routine, just without Má. No funeral to attend. No gathering to share memories. No closure. Our family in Winnipeg was all on my dad's side. My cousins did not share my loss. My cousin on my mom's side reached out from California. Her parents were on their way to Vietnam too. She and her sister, my sister and I, separated but united in our grief. Still, my grief had nowhere to land, nowhere to go. So it leaked out of me, in surprising tears at the oddest moments—a meeting at work, on the bus ride home, watching TV with my boyfriend. Was my grief enough? Was it too much? I was bits and pieces of grief, not knowing if I was the right mix.

Should I light incense on Ba's altar for Bà Ngoại? Would that be too confusing for their spirits? Would that be against the rules? Would the spirits of Ba and Bà Ngoại be offended? In the movies, people would go to a grand church and light a candle. What were the rituals I could perform? Faced with grief and uncertainty, this was the time people relied the most on their faith, to help them through moments of darkness and pain. A sense of loss or untethering. This was the moment I felt my lack of faith the most.

* * *

The monk at Bà Ngoại's altar clutched a yellow carnation in one hand and a glass of water in the other. He marched around each family member, dipped the carnation in the water, and flicked the water at each person in turn with another twist of his wrist.

I questioned the rituals.

I was not a believer.

But this was when I knew I wanted to be a believer.

Grasping and falling and failing. I knew I needed something more, something as an anchor for my life. Trưng Trắc was the beginning. I was grateful for that connection. But it wasn't enough. I needed more.

This moment became the spark for my search for faith.

I returned to myself. The water was cool on my head and neck, soothing me and grounding me. Maybe we were washing ourselves of mourning. Purification. The monk told us to strip out of our mourning clothes. I took off my white headband and the feel of the fabric lingered on my skin.

The monk directed the family to dismantle the altar and take down the picture. The candles, the incense, and the plates of food disappeared into the kitchen in the hands of various cousins. All physical reminders of mourning, of grief, were to be cast off and burned.

After the ceremony, we travelled to Bà Ngoại's gravesite in a caravan of cars, white mourning clothes in the back of one van. Bà Ngoại was buried in the cemetery near the village where she grew up. I walked past mud and bamboo leaves, tin-roofed houses, chickens and cows, and bare-chested children.

We reached her resting place. The gravesite was not as I imagined it would be. There was a grey stone tomb big enough to accommodate the coffin. At the head of the tomb were two stone pillars with pink lotus blossoms on top. At the foot of the tomb was her headstone, Chinese characters carved into the granite. I wondered why her name wasn't written in Vietnamese.

My mind focussed on Bà Ngoại. She lived in Vietnam her entire life. When Má made her monthly calls to Bà Ngoại, I cringed when she beckoned me to the blue plastic phone. "Bà Ngoại khỏe không?" was all I ever said. Are you well grandma? I heard the need in her voice for something more. What she wanted from me, I could not give her.

At her gravesite, I thought back to my second trip to Vietnam, when I was sixteen. Bà Ngoại and I would sit together on the stone bench outside her house, watching the market right outside her doorstep. My aunt sold small household items like toothbrushes, towels, shampoo and dried foods at the front of the house. A woman stopped by on a rusty bike, her toddler holding her waist on a makeshift seat behind her. She bought two bundles of rice paper, balancing them on her handlebars as she spoke to my aunt. Bà Ngoại nodded at the woman; she knew her as she knew everyone who stopped by.

Bà Ngoại radiated a force of will just with her presence, sharp eyes, and bright face. Everyone turned when she spoke, made room when she moved. She chewed green leaves and spat them in a bronze spittoon, her mouth dark red and teeth stained by the betel-nut juice. She had a habit of loosening her bun, shaking out her silvery white hair almost down to her waist, and remaking it. If she thought I was cold, she covered my shoulders with a blanket, and asked if I was hungry or thirsty. Bà Ngoại's shining eyes and bright face, her love for me when I didn't even know her, I miss all of it. Blood to blood, kin to kin, her spirit to my spirit.

Tears bubbled up and broke free. I cried. I cried for all the times I couldn't find the tears. My Ba. My Bà Ngoại. I held my arms in front of me, clasped together in front.

My uncle made a funeral pyre of the mourning clothes and the other items behind Bà Ngoại's tomb. Smoke rose up to the afterlife. The mourning period had ended.

The incense continued to burn.

The wind dried the tears on my face.

* * *

A week after I stood at Bà Ngoại's gravesite, Má and Jen and I went on tour. Not growing up here, I had so many questions and uncertainties about my Vietnamese-ness. Previous trips were about visiting relatives, splitting time between Trảng Bàng and Sài Gòn, spending the majority of time in the homes of various family members. In and out of air-conditioned taxis and vans to stare at the same few walls of my relatives' homes.

On this trip, I had the deep need (and financial means finally) to explore more of the land where I was born. What a difference to be immersed in Vietnamese-ness. I did not have to explain myself. That was a burden I set down for a few weeks. A breath I let out for a while. Was that why Má didn't do explanations? She needed to set down that burden?

Here, Buddhist temples were more prevalent than Christian churches. Monks walked along the road in their saffron robes. Altars to ancestors were tucked in corners in restaurants, shops, and in people's houses. Ashes blew off the tile floors into the wind. Offerings of fruit and food were always present. There were market stands to buy joss sticks of every scent, replacement bulbs for plastic candles, paper ghost money—everything one could need for an altar.

I had to make an effort to learn about Vietnam. I knew a lot about Thanksgiving and Remembrance Day. But I knew very little about International Women's Day (a major celebration in Vietnam) and Tết. I knew a lot about British monarchs and the American Revolution. I knew very little about French colonialism in Vietnam or the Nguyên Dynasty.

I felt more like I belonged, and yet, I was reminded that I was still separate. While I internalized Vietnam, Vietnamese people on the street still saw me as different. I was not allowed to forget that fact. They still looked at each other and stated "Việt Kiều" as I passed. Even if I got closer, I was never on the inside.

I was in Hà Nội, steps away from the Hát river where the Trưng sisters fought their last battle. I envisioned their last stand. The sisters rode side by side each one on the back of an enormous elephant decorated with war paint and showing off bloodied tusks. Both women had their swords drawn. Trắc raised her sword above her head wanting her troops to be able to see she was well and steady in the face of fear, to fortify their own hearts. The sunlight reflected brightly off the sharp metal, a flash of heaven on earth— Nhị pointed her sword straight in front, her hand firm, signalling attack. The enemy was advancing, a shadow stretching across the field, the earth shuddering under thousands of footfalls and hooves.

Upon the grasslands, a soldier had fallen, locks of her hair loosened from her braid, her face turned up to the clear sky. Another soldier screamed as the front of her tunic was soaked by a wound in her chest. Black birds circled; the air was thick with tiny flecks of blood still suspended above the ground. Soldiers fell. Dark earth churned with hot crimson blood.

Trắc and Nhị were on foot after being tumbled from their elephants, swords tossed to the earth in haste. The rhythm of the river was calling to them. Waiting to embrace them for eternity.

"Sister!" Nhị called out to Trắc, stretching her arms out to her.

"We will be together again, sister!" Trắc responded as she reached the water's edge.

The Trưng sisters passed from this world into the spirit world.

Trưng Trắc watches from the otherworld. Her influence and her power burn bright. The Trưng sisters live on as the spirits of Vietnamese freedom and feminism. Today, they continue their reign from the afterlife in Vietnam, as temples, shrines, statues, streets, buildings, and an annual festival, all bear their names. Whispers of their reappearance and intervention in the lives of emperors and ordinary folk alike have also been passed down for centuries. Throughout Vietnam and other places in the world where Vietnamese people have put down roots, people cúng to the Trưng sisters, offering what they have and praying for what they do not have.

As I walked the dusty streets of downtown Hà Nội, was Trưng Trắc's spirit peeking around the next banyan tree? Did her spirit linger where she fell? The blood that was spilled here two thousand years ago seeped deep into the earth and nourished the land season after season, telling its own tale year after year. I was walking that earth. I was now a part of that story.

In Vietnam I collected rocks, a habit I started in university. Around the banks of the Lake of the Restored Sword, I picked up a nickel-size rock, a shade of off-white, flat on one side and jagged on the other side. Perhaps this rock was part of the bedrock thousands of years ago at the bottom of the lake, gradually pushed upward over many decades, churned in the water, broken up and eroded to the point it became a stone and washed up on the banks, waiting to reveal itself to me to bring it back to Winnipeg. I brought back a piece of Trưng Trắc's story to add to my own story. Trưng Trắc opened the door. Before, the way was barred to me.

I felt a spark that started with the Trưng sisters, one bright star in the night sky. The heavens were filled with stars, filled with heroes and the legends and legacies they left behind. The stars had a long history, light travelled through space to brighten Earth's sky, but the light from these giant balls could have taken thousands of years to travel. Perhaps the stars I focussed on no longer existed; instead they were echoes of bright moments in time that were long over. The stars were reaching through time, not just space. Like the spirits of my ancestors reaching from ten years ago, or 100 years ago, or 2000 years ago. I was able to walk the same earth in the country they once walked. I studied the night sky in the same place on earth they did. I still saw their light.

Was it my own weakness or was it my strength—my need to question? True faith is blind faith. Would faith come easier to me if I was different, if I didn't question and just accepted? Was I making the journey, the search, harder on myself? Did I put up my own obstacles? This space in-between felt like an emptiness, a hunger, a mirage. If I was bits and pieces of material, I began to realize I would need to collect threads to be able to stitch myself together.

A crack in the window, a doorway not quite shut, a lid slightly ajar. Enough of an opening through which
light may pass,

air may flow,

water may seep,

and spirit may come.

* * *

In my Ông Nội's house in Trảng Bàng, on the second floor, there is also an altar to Ba. In the house where my dad grew up, perhaps even in the very same room he had shared with his brothers, his parents had set up his altar on a shiny wooden chest.

A few days before we left to come back to Canada, after our tour of the country, I sat with Ba.

I came here to end the mourning period for Bà Ngoại. I should not have been surprised to meet Ba here as well. In Vietnam, family was everywhere, both in the land of the living and the land beyond. I thought I had left Ba at our house in Winnipeg and yet I stared at the familiar eyes from the same black and white picture behind glass.

His parents, my Ông Nội and my Bà Nội, never saw him alive again after wishing him well on his journey to Canada. What had been the cost to them? To say goodbye to their first-born child, a beloved and devoted son, and give him up to the unknown? How did they react when they heard the news he had died across the ocean and they would never see him again in this lifetime? Perhaps they wailed and sobbed, or perhaps they swallowed their sorrow like Má, or turned numb, like I had.

Did Ông Nội and Bà Nội speak to him too? Did he reside in Winnipeg or in Trảng Bàng or both? As a spirit, perhaps space and physical location were meaningless, a constructs of the mind. Freed from his body, he was energy and light.

Sitting there, feeling Ba close to me, I knew I wanted to invite faith into my life. I knew I was incomplete, that I needed more, that I needed to find the material to bind myself together. I would not be a fake any longer.

I went to Vietnam thinking I would learn more about my own culture and identity. It surprised me that by being in Vietnam, this experience became the impetus to want to explore other traditions around the world. I had a rich foundation. Without strong roots, I could not have grown.

By immersing myself in faith more deeply in Vietnam, this ignited the curiosity for something new. If Vietnam had so much to be discovered, I could only imagine what the rest of the world held. A journey to the land of my ancestors provided the launching point to seek the spiritual in other traditions in other parts of the world. I was ready to travel to places I had been dreaming about since I was a kid.

I took a cloth from the kitchen and swept away the ashes on Ba's altar, sweeping away last month's prayers and wishes.

Two: Sacred Spaces and Legends

GOING TO VIETNAM for the end of the mourning period for Bà Ngoại lit a spark in me to explore other traditions across the globe. This was the right time to travel—I was in my mid-twenties and working full-time, with enough vacation time and savings to do so. In creating my itineraries, one of my goals was to travel to the spaces that spoke the most to my heart: to walk the earth, to breathe the air, and to bear witness to the divine. Since childhood, I had stepped into the glossy pages of my oversized books, imagining casting my shadow in the photos and drawings. I read about and dreamt about places where history and mythology merge. I would search for and collect the threads I needed to begin to stitch myself together.

Sacred spaces have called to humans throughout millennia, to pray, to meditate, build places of worship, and to connect to spirit. I wanted to experience how spirituality manifests in cultures and traditions around the world. While vast differences exist, what struck me most were the parallels. There are parallels in the stories we tell each other and in the stories that are passed down through the generations. In travelling to different spaces, I witnessed similar stories told repeatedly. My childhood need to question faith evolved into my adult quest to understand what the parallel stories revealed to me about my own life. This quest led to more questions, questions I may spend my life pondering, questions philosophers, theologians, and seekers have asked through the generations.

One parallel is about monarchs peering beyond this life and preparing for the next life. As I explored their stories, I wondered what happened to their afterlives when their eternal slumber was disturbed?

Thinking about them opened the door for me to think about my own mortality and what happens after. What will happen when I pass from this life?

* * *

Pharaoh Khufu was a man obsessed, concerned with his eternal life beyond this one. During the time period he ruled Egypt, he built the Great Pyramid, enabling an ascent to heaven, as far away from the earth as possible. The pyramid was meant to last an eternity, to protect Pharaoh's human body so his spirits could recognize it and be reunited in the land beyond the living.

He was buried with jewellery, gold and coin, food and wine, clothing and toiletries, boats and chariots. All he would need in the afterlife, after his body was mummified and laid to rest, he brought with him.

When the sun set on his mortal life, he would take the journey through endless night.

Emperor Qin, China's first Emperor, believed in life beyond death. In this world, he worked towards his vision of a united middle kingdom. He cast his eyes far beyond the veil that separated the living and the dead and plotted his rule over the shadows of the underworld. If he was to be a mighty monarch in the shadow world, what would he need with him?

He was buried with archers, and foot soldiers, generals and swordsmen, leaders and followers, horses and chariots. He designed a great palace through which to walk the grounds for eternity. He had all he needed with him.

When the sun set on his mortal life, he would take the journey through endless night.

* * *

While the spirits of Vietnam have always enchanted me, the attraction to Egypt is equally strong; my heartbeat quickens as I daydream of the goddesses and gods walking alongside humans—their connection so direct. While the land of my birth is an anchor of rituals and traditions rooted in memory, Egypt evokes the unfamiliar yet wondrous, the possibilities waiting to be embraced. Egypt – the land of Isis and Osiris, Ra and Nut – an ancient desert land that gave birth to a spiritual tradition thousands of years ago. It's a land that calls to seekers of the sacred—like me.

As a kid reading about ancient Egypt late into the night, I imagined myself visiting the pyramids. The heat of mid-day creating the shimmering effect of a mirage. Shifting on a camel, the glittering sand blowing all around. Was this a dream or was it real? Was I in my room in Winnipeg staring at a glossy picture, visualizing I was walking through the page into the desert, or was I a grown woman living out my fantasy in a hazy delirium?

Here I was making my way by camel towards the pyramids of Giza, riding in a small herd with our tour group. Each camel was led on foot by a local man, his face and mouth wrapped in cloth a barrier against the blowing sand. I named my camel Tawny, deciding she was a female because of her curly eyelashes. She was the shade of golden-brown sugar and as she cocked her huge head to the side I told her she was a smart camel and a pretty camel. She kept butting her head into the side of the camel carrying my husband Ryan, wanting the attention of both beast and man. Perhaps they were life partners, these two camels, like Ryan and me.

I had not expected that Ryan and I would get together. When we first met in university, in business school, I had told myself no more dating, just focus on school. After spending the first year of university obsessing over securing a boyfriend, which resulted in a few false starts, gossip, and tears, I swore second year would be different. Then I met Ryan and it all changed. Ryan and I – both born in the year of the Rooster only four months apart, in different countries, born into different cultures, different religions, different socio-economic conditions—were pulled together in the centre of Canada.

His brown hair, usually cropped short to his head, fair skin and sharp nose reflect his English and Scottish heritage. His green eyes speckled with gold scan a room and note the details. With the kind of mind that is endlessly calculating, value is always the fundamental question and forms the foundation for his decision making. Ryan once told me that if we ever have twins, they wouldn't wear matching outfits, because why would we buy two of everything? They could share the same wardrobe and we would spend the money we saved on clothes on something else—stretching the value of the garments. He is always five minutes early. Never forgets to call his mom and dad on their birthdays. He does what he says and says what he does. I wonder if he and Ba would have gotten along.

"Well?" he asked, turning around on his camel, to face me. His long-sleeve linen button-up shirt was the same shade as the desert sand as it flapped in the breeze.

I smiled, giddy, and still in shock. "It's even better." I shouted between Tawny's pointed ears.

Ryan turned to face forward again and nodded, satisfied. He knew what it meant to me to be here.

As we made our approach, the three pyramids lined up in a beautifully symmetrical diagonal line, inviting us closer, a deliberate mathematical design. What appeared smooth and sloping from afar were revealed as jagged blocks of stones up close, like LEGO blocks fitted together, edges exposed in a zigzag design upward. The limestone casing around the entire structure had been stripped; it was no longer a glittering diamond in the desert.

I exhaled the breath I did not realize I was holding. The inside of my nose felt prickly with the dry heat. My focus shifted between the panoramic view of azure skies and dusty monuments to zoom in on the curve of the rock and dark shadows of crumbled stone. I inhaled, attempting to capture this moment, this feeling. How did humankind manifest such testaments to their faith?

How could I embrace the moment when it pushed the boundaries of my experiences, when it existed along the edges of human comprehension, to know the gods? It felt like my heart would not be enough to contain the awe and joy I felt standing here, witnessing this moment.

Ryan leaned over his camel to hand the camera to one of the guides who then took our picture with the pyramids in the background.

"And now kiss," the guide ordered, camera in hand for another shot.

Ryan tasted like lip balm and home.

Tears threatened to escape behind my sunglasses. We were celebrating our third wedding anniversary on this trip in Egypt, fulfilling a childhood dream that I wouldn't have had the courage for on my own. Ryan had made it happen for me; he was the momentum I needed to move beyond my static state. Ryan could push me past my edges and enable me to collect the threads I needed to stitch myself together.

The largest pyramid, known as the Great Pyramid, is the resting place of Pharaoh Khufu. Khufu died after his ka, his life energy, left his body. During the Opening of the Mouth ceremony performed after death, his ba, his unique personality, was released in the form of a human-headed bird. His ba and ka parts of his soul found reunification as the Akh in the afterlife. Khufu journeyed with the sun each day to reunite with Osiris in the underworld each night. As I got off my camel, I wondered if Pharaoh's ba was fluttering around his final resting place, searching, as his body no longer rested here.

After Pharaoh had been sealed up in his burial mound, spells were cast as a warning. Prophecies foretold of great misfortune befalling all who sought wealth and who spat on the gods. Yet the pyramids were beacons, announcing the treasure within and sadly the tombs were opened, and the riches looted. Greed triumphed over faith. The tragedy that befell archeologist Howard Carter and others who disturbed the tomb of Pharaoh Tutankhamun reinforced the mummy's curse. I wondered, how did Pharaoh exist in the afterlife without his earthly treasures?

Walking the perimeter of the Great Pyramid, built over four thousand years ago, I could not help but feel like a speck in time and space, a dust particle floating in air, glinting off sunlight. Not just human lives, but entire civilizations had flourished and were forgotten in that time frame. I closed my eyes and tried to bottle this feeling to carry home to Winnipeg to uncork the next time I was stressed about a work deadline or fretted over a missed workout. Live in the moment, why stress? What would remain of me, in four thousand years, that mattered? These were the threads I collected in the desert sands—a perspective of myself as stardust in the night sky.

* * *

A year after going to Egypt, Ryan and I travelled to China. We visited the tomb of Emperor Qin. Marriage continued to be a balm, smoothing the edges of my insecurities and questions while creating space for me to figure out my faith. Anchored by Vietnamese spirituality, I stretched and reached and meandered to different lands and different traditions that called to me. Both my grandfathers left China as young men and built lives for themselves in Vietnam. Chinese history and mythology are inextricably linked to Vietnamese history and mythology, as they are linked to my family's story.

Over two thousand years ago, Emperor Qin buried thousands of terra cotta warriors to accompany him to the afterlife. It had been the greatest journey to travel and the greatest adventure to embark upon. Having conquered this life, he had gazed ahead to the next challenge, to the next conquest. What compelled him? Was it fear of an ending? Or the excitement of a new beginning? Was it faith that the afterlife would be as he imagined, as he planned? The moments before his death, did he wonder what would come next?

"Ryan, stand right there."

I knelt behind him and swiped a rock from Pit 1, the largest pit found at Emperor Qin's tomb in Xi'an. I was continuing my ritual of collecting rocks from around the world.

He nodded patiently, resigned to my thieving ways.

Pit 1 looked like it was the size of a football field, with rows and rows of soldiers. The hundreds, maybe thousands, of other tourists surrounding us enveloped me in heartbeats, footfalls, chattering voices, and flashing cameras, all creating a frantic energy.

The Emperor's terracotta army also made their presence known via their stances, their intense glances, and their unwavering attention. They had been created to guard over royalty, and so they did, even after thousands of years. I stood with my hands on the railing and I stared at them and they all stared back at me, unblinking.

Some were tall, some were short, some were slim, and some appeared well-fed. There were kneeling archers, standing archers, infantry, officers, generals, and charioteers. Role and rank were evident from each man's uniform. The colour had faded from the warriors—once unsealed—from tanned faces with blue or green or red clothes to dusty grey. Over 6,000 men, all broken before, had been restored. Some were left broken as a memorial to the army's state when the tomb was opened. Broken faces, torsos, limbs striking out, noses peeking through, buried under sand and rock. This wasn't an army of clones, from a factory mould, marked "Made in China." It was an army of individuals. Each one of them was carved by an artist and given an expression. I stared into the stone eyes of many as we walked through the various chambers. They could have been modelled after real men. Perhaps real men who had served the Emperor in life had given their images to serve beyond their own lifetime, breathing their energy into the clay, sending them into the future.

Ryan and I said we would start trying for a baby after this vacation. As I looked at the individual soldiers, I daydreamed about the baby Ryan and I would have, about what our child would look like. Would the baby be chubby with rolls around wrists and ankles, inheriting Ryan's nose and my chin? The baby would be a piece of me living beyond myself, like the men in front of me.

Local farmers had originally discovered the burial mound in the 1970s, as they were drilling wells in search of water. The day we visited the tomb, one of those farmers was there signing autographs. The farmer wore a dark blue linen jacket and thick glasses but had tanned skin and a slim build. A simple farmer still. As I waited in line to get his signature on our copy of the tourist book produced locally, I noticed a slight touch of melancholy in the hunch of his shoulders and in the way he curled the characters of his name in Chinese. A sign served as a barrier between him and us, "No pictures No questions." I wanted to ask him if he was haunted by any of the terra cotta soldiers. Had Emperor Qin visited him in his dreams, asking, "Why do you disturb my slumber?" As he was forever linked to the opening of the burial of a king, did a shadow of a curse follow the farmer?

* * *

Pharaoh Khufu and Emperor Qin both built elaborate burial tombs, in accordance with their faith. Yet their tombs were never intended to be found.

We are the modern-day tomb robbers—the archeologists excavating the eternal resting places of these kings, and seekers like me, well intentioned with only curiosity and reverence in our hearts.

Is memory not the afterlife? I wondered. Is the afterlife not a remembrance by those still in the land of the living? Pharaoh Khufu lives beyond death. Emperor Qin lives beyond death. If we, generation after generation, do not visit the tombs, write about the wonders, take and share photographs, create paintings and sculptures, memories to hold onto, the names and the deeds of these monarchs would fade into history, into darkness, and be forgotten by all. And as we hold onto them, we hold onto their belief systems. Their wishes are fulfilled. Through human memory, carried forward from person to person, we ensure that they reach out beyond death. As the Trưng sisters had already reached out beyond death to me.

Is that not what I do for Ba and for Bà Ngoại—ensure they do not fade? But do they have what they need in the realm of the spirits? Do they get the offerings of food we send them through the incense? Do I ensure their continued existence? By celebrating their death anniversaries each year and cúnging to them, do their spirits slip in between worlds?

What will I bring over to the afterlife? Will anyone cúng to me? What burial rites will I choose for my family members to observe in my honour?

What do I believe will be my afterlife?

I have been blessed to bear witness to the manifestations of life after death in Egypt and in China. I have explored the wondrous and grand ideas humans conjure up when faced with mortality and the black void of death. These are the stories we tell ourselves. The afterlife is an integral part of life and spirit in cultures and societies all around the world. Travelling to these places, collecting the threads, invited me to ponder the universal question:

What happens at the end?

* * *

Pharaoh Khufu and Emperor Qin passed into the realm of legend, becoming more than historical figures, fact interwoven into folklore. The legend of the Trưng sisters, fact and myth intertwined, speaks to Vietnamese feminism and independence. The realm of legend is crowded with heroes. A hero could be one historical figure or a compilation of a few different figures over a period of time. It's not the truth of the heroes that has been holding my heart captive, it's the stories themselves and what they mean for us.

How did these heroes who achieved great feats, wielding magical instruments on loan from divine entities, conduct themselves? How did they use what tools were given to them to be the best versions of themselves? As I explored their stories, I wondered what I may learn from the heroes of the past and apply to my own life. What is my purpose in life? These may be questions I ponder my whole life.

Lê Lợi was the leader of the army in Vietnam, sworn to cast off the Chinese invaders from his land. A fisherman-turned-solider found a sword tangled in his nets one day and gave it to his commander Lê Lợi. Lê Lợi knew this was his sign from heaven and named the sword Will of Heaven. After ten years of war, he was able to drive away the Chinese army. He crowned himself Emperor Lê Thái Tổ, first of the Lê Dynasty.

Arthur, the son of Uther Pendragon, pulled the sword from the stone to fulfill the prophecy that he was the rightful king of Britain. Or was Excalibur presented to him by the Lady of the Lake? He ruled over Camelot with Queen Guinevere. He founded the Knights of the Round Table, so that no man sat at the head of the table, but all men were equal. His mentor was Merlin. Among his adventures and honourable deeds, he defended his realm from Saxon invaders.

Years later, Emperor Lê was on his boat on a lake when the Golden Tortoise emerged and expressed to the Emperor it was time to return the Will of Heaven to its true owner, the Dragon King. Emperor Lê placed the sword into the mouth of the tortoise and both disappeared into the water.

Years later, King Arthur was mortally wounded and was brought to the Isle of Avalon in a barge. Along the way, Excalibur was flung into the deep water. The Lady of the Lake reached out her arm and grabbed the sword, taking it back to its watery home.

Destiny fulfilled. The sword was returned

Destiny fulfilled. The sword was returned.

* * *

A week after the end of the mourning period for Bà Ngoại, Má and Jen and I went on tour in Vietnam. The day we visited Hồ Hoàn Kiếm—the famous Lake of the Restored Sword—in Hà Nội, the humidity was so tangible it was like a warm shawl draped over my shoulders, water droplets in the air woven tightly together. It was hard to move, hard to breathe.

I stared out at the waves of emerald water sparkling in the sunlight. Emperor Lê had Turtle Tower built on an island in the middle of the lake. The tower was carved from grey stone now covered by a light dusting of moss, the roof topped with terracotta tiles that curved at the ends like a curly moustache. The tower looked like it was floating, hovering just above the green glass of the lake.

Jen and I sat by ourselves on the stone bench overlooking the lake. We had been sitting in silence for a while, neither of us wanting to speak first, both of us too stubborn to do so.

Our conversations could go sideways so quickly. This time, we were bickering about plans and interpreting intentions and yet it was never just about the current thing, it was always about every other interaction over our years together.

Strangers always thought Jen and I were twins when they first met us together. I did not find this amusing as she is seven years older. But we shared the same facial features, dark bob, and mannerisms. She embodied the heroic Trưng Trắc to me, even off the stage. My sister was my best friend and my harshest critic. She was my mirror; we reflected each other's strengths and reflected each other's failings.

I breathed out and my anger dissolved a bit. It was difficult to hold onto it when we were surrounded by serenity. If we stayed in this stalemate, we would miss more of the day.

I blinked first; I usually did. "Fine, we'll go where you want."

She nodded. "Ok, let's go."

Jen and I didn't say sorry to each other. We didn't acknowledge hurt feelings, we just moved on. We carried our invisible backpacks, heavy with old hurts, words that we could never take back, and moments when we had disappointed each other.

Jen started walking around the lake and I followed her.

The lotus blossoms along the edge of the lake, vibrant pink, opened in the sun, beauty emerging from dirt and darkness. I gazed at Turtle Tower through the curtain of flowers drooping over from the trees, the branches sighing in the wind's caress, and my shoulders started to soften, pulling away from my ears.

Emperor Lê had returned his magical object here. The sword was no longer needed. The sword may be at the bottom of this lake, in the palace of the Dragon King. When the Will of Heaven was given back, was the Emperor saddened to be parted from it? Or was he relieved of its burden, the weight of power? It was never his, it was lent to him to do what he must, and then to be set aside.

By renaming the lake after the restored sword, the Emperor marked the passage from aggression to peace, laying aside the weapon. He marked the time for restoration. The Emperor built what was needed—the foundation for a gathering place. On this spot, family and friends, arms linked, laughing and listening, circle the lake, a sign of community and vitality.

As Jen and I continued walking, I wondered if having the sword by his side gave Emperor Lê a sense of invincibility, made him hold his head up higher, speak with more conviction, make life decisions with more confidence. With the sword as his talisman, as his connection to the divine, he was more than mortal. The sword gave him the power to rise up to be a better person, to fulfill his ultimate potential, to become the best version of himself.

I did not wield a sword infused with magic and power, but I did need things—words, tools, and perspectives that could possibly support me. I was still collecting the pieces to help me become my best self. I strove to be kinder to Jen and kinder to Má and kinder to myself. I aspired to achieve great deeds in my own life as I defined that—to be of service, to have an impact, to be a positive influence.

The wind blew the rubied blossoms off the tree branches into the water and the jewels scattered. The breeze was cool on my face and arms, the scent of roses and wet earth tickling my nose. I smiled and linked my arm through Jen's.

* * *

Years later, Jen and I were travelling, just the two of us, through England, Scotland, and France. After I had married and moved out of the house, we'd had to redefine our relationship, figure out how to make time for each other, the busyness of life separating us. Neither of us wanted to grow apart, but it took a conscious effort to remain close. This trip was a way to slow down, to listen to each other, and to get to know in more depth who we were growing into.

It was windy the day we visited the Tor in Glastonbury, England. I stood where the Isle of Avalon was believed to be, where King Arthur was brought at the end of his days and buried. The stairs cut into the earth were like segments of a serpent slithering from side to side up the steep hill, leading me closer to the heavens. The grass was lush, hairs covering the earth, tickling the air. I began my ascent in search of the King, my eyes on the step in front of me and the step after that and the step after that. My shoes were proper running shoes, grey and ventilated at the top. This time, I'd sacrificed fashion for practicality. My body was changing, shifting as I was gaining weight in my chest and in my abdomen, and I could not predict my sense of balance. I had my hands in my jacket, escaping the gusts. I rubbed my hands over my just-into-second trimester pregnancy bump. Firm and rounded and reassuring. This was my delicious secret from most of the world as I was not showing yet. My body felt different to me, heavy, of substance. New life and new potential. Jen followed a few footfalls behind me, ready to catch me if my centre of gravity proved unreliable.

This sister trip before the baby came made me think of my childhood summers when it was up to Jen to watch me, to entertain me. Má was always working. There were no costly summer camps or elaborate family vacations when I was a kid. Instead, Jen and I spent the summers laughing and arguing. Jen took me on bus adventures to different parts of the city, different libraries, holding my hand between her flexible fingers. When she could drive and we finally had a family car, a used car a relative let us drive, we embarked on car adventures to the different Value Villages around the city, seeking the best book deals. It was years before Google Maps. Before Kijiji.

One summer, we went on an "adventure" to Eaton's downtown. I know I was in grade six or seven because we still lived in the green rental house on Beverley Street. I was looking at all the Barbie doll clothes. I was obsessing over a beautiful outfit, deep purple overcoat, purple beret, black knee-high boots and black scarf with a swirly design.

"I really really want it." I said as I hugged the plastic packaging to my chest.

"We don't have enough money."

"How much is it?" I pleaded.

"More than we have. We're going to get a Big Mac meal and Happy Meal at McDonald's."

"What if we don't eat?"

"You're not hungry?"

I clutched the package on the bus on the way home and couldn't wait to put it on my perfect blonde Barbie doll. We had shared a small order of fries, although Jen let me eat most of them.

With that memory in my mind, I looked back at Jen and we both smiled. The magic of King Arthur had always enchanted us both. We both knew how much it meant to share this moment together in Glastonbury. At the top, the stone tower of St. Michael's chapel greeted us. The Isle of Avalon used to be surrounded by water, by a lake. There was a veil of mists that concealed the magical Isle. The water had vanished long ago, leaving behind emerald lands and swaying trees, some glittering in the bright light, some dark in the shadow of clouds. Under a dome of sapphire skies and opal clouds, I felt alive and awake. I was happily caught between this world and the realm above us, suspended between reality and legend.

A hero was buried here. I had come to Glastonbury intentionally to occupy the same space that King Arthur had passed through. Here was an echo of a legend. A link to the tale was forged here. The winds blew my hair across my face and dust into my eyes, the gusts swirling through time and space. If I looked hard enough, would my gaze pierce through the veils and the mists surrounding Avalon?

I envisioned King Arthur and wondered how many other seekers thought of him while standing on the Tor. Did the fact that so many people contemplated his essence in this concentrated space give the King form again, rising from the past, from the realm of legend? Did he cross over into our realm to be a source of inspiration to artists, writers, storytellers, filmmakers? When he was parted from Excalibur, his source of power, did the weight come off his shoulders, no longer burdened by expectations to do great deeds? He was a vessel to carry out what the universe intended to unfold. His legend grew, changed, adapted to the times, reflected the context, became what a hero needed to be. Would his deeds inspire those who visited here to be heroes in their own lives?

***

I have been blessed to bear witness to heroes who fulfilled their destinies in Vietnam and in England. Magical swords wielded and returned, and the power of water to call to that magic were signs that they were carrying out the will of the universe with divine assistance. The men no longer remain but the legends remain. And importantly, the stories we tell ourselves remain.

What is my sword, my instrument through which I make my contribution to the world? When did I receive a gift from the keepers of the secrets, the vanguards of the natural order, those mystical all-seeing beings that interfere with a human's life? And how will I know to return it so that it may be called for another purpose? Everything has a season. And then it passes.

What great deeds can I aspire to in my relationships, in my work, in my community? When I enter motherhood, how will I inspire the next generation?

Travelling to these places, collecting the threads:

How am I the heroine in my story?

* * *

Pharaoh Khufu and Emperor Qin chose the sites for their burial grounds. Emperor Lê and King Arthur were compelled to act in specific locations. What was unique about these places on earth? Why were these spaces the thresholds to step into eternity?

The Golden Tortoise asked Emperor Lê for the return of the sword when the Emperor was out on the lake. The Golden Tortoise was instrumental in choosing the location that would be commemorated in the future. I knew of other divine creatures who also played a role in the origins of sacred spaces.

As I explored their stories, I wondered about my own beginnings. What may I learn from the origins of these sites that I may apply to my own life? Where do I come from? What is the story of where I started? How does my beginning influence how I live my life? These may be questions I ponder my whole life.

* * *

Eagles were significant to Zeus as his symbol and sacred animal. From his throne on Mount Olympus in Greece, Zeus feasted on nectar and ambrosia, while interfering in the lives of mortals. The king of the gods wanted to find the centre of the world. Where was the physical location on earth that represented the navel of the world—the spot that connected earth to heaven, the umbilical cord tethering the two together? The spot that signified creation and the source of life. And signified no beginning and no ending, timeless.

To carry out his goal, he had two eagles released at the same time. One flew from the western end of the world and one flew from the eastern end of the world. They travelled at the same speed towards each other. Where they met after encircling the world was the centre. That place was Delphi in Greece. Located on the south-western slope of Mount Parnassus, overlooking deep valleys of olive trees, a few hours north of Athens, a religious complex was built.

Eagles ascended above the clouds.

Dragons are part of the origin story of the Vietnamese people. We are descendants of the union between a fairy and a dragon. The dragon brings the rain on the rice fields, fertility and life. The dragon is the symbol of the Emperor. Vietnamese dragons are different from European dragons depicted with great bellies, long necks, and massive wings. Vietnamese dragons are long and lean, with thin arms and legs, and wispy beards and scales along their backs. They glide through the air as an eel would move through the water, slithering one way and then the other.

When the Chinese army was preparing to strike in northern Vietnam, the gods sent a family of dragons from heaven to help the people defend the land. The dragons spat out jewels and jade pieces that turned into the islands along the bay, creating a barrier to the invaders. The dragons were so enchanted by the calm water and the reverence of the people, they decided to stay. Where the dragons descended became Hạ Long Bay.

Dragons descended into the sea.

* * *

When Ryan and I travelled to Egypt, we also went to Greece as part of the same trip. Greek mythology had also left its mark on me as a child; with its tales of love and miracles, tragedy and heartbreak, how close goddesses and gods were to humans. I felt compelled to seek out the deities in their homeland.

To mark the spot of the "the navel of the earth," or omphalos, as revealed by his eagles, Zeus threw a stone down from the sky—the navel stone. This stone is believed to be the same stone that Zeus' mom Rhea wrapped in cloth to trick her husband Cronus to swallow in the place of the infant Zeus. Through the navel stone, the invisible link of the umbilical cord stretches from earth to heaven. An object, and also a location, the naval stone represents the centre, not of the physical dimension of the world, but it's centeredness between earth and sky, mortal and divine, eternity.

Outside Apollo's Temple in Delphi, I placed both my hands on the dome-shaped naval stone. Cool and coarse, it felt gritty against my fingertips. My hands glistened with sweat and sunscreen, skin lightly tanned—active life resting against still rock. I was surprised it was not roped off like much of the rest of the complex, perhaps because it was a replica of the one placed there centuries ago. The naval stone sat on a square stone base and reached to the height of my chest. At its base, two people would be able to encircle it in their arms and at its height, I would be able cover it with just my hand. The stone was a greyish beige, with criss-cross marks like scars or arteries and veins, circulating the essence of the universe.

I imagined all the hands of all the people who had come this way. I smiled, comforted by my connection to all seekers. Did we leave behind part of ourselves, flesh on stone, an imprint of our life histories? Or did we take away with us part of the navel stone, a thread that bound us to the cosmic beginning? A cosmic thread attached at the top and at the bottom, reaching away from each other for so long the two points eventually met. I had made my personal connection to the navel stone that was a link between realms.

I was at the centre. The beginning and the ending and the beginning again.

I wanted to continue to unmask the divine at each sacred space I visited, pulling a thread from the earth to add to my collection, and weave them to bind me together.

As I stood trying to hold the view from the mountain top in my memory, the view evoked divinity with the green valley breathing, the collective inhaling and exhaling of each leaf and blade of grass. Olive trees stretching roots and standing tall, toward the sun and the skies. Mountain slopes folded behind each other, retreating to the horizon, cloud and sky behind that. Sculpted by nature to be the perfect spot for worship. Between heaven and earth, suspended. The sun was high above the earth, Apollo in his chariot travelling across the sky, cloudless and calm, paradise on earth. From here, could I see the eagles of Zeus circle and soar?

* * *

On the same tour that Má and Jen and I took in Vietnam after the end of the mourning period for Bà Ngoại, we travelled from Hà Nội to Hạ Long Bay. Sitting in a boat on the bay, I was mesmerized by the cobalt clear water rippling across the crystal surface. Jagged grey limestone peaks emerged from the depths. Luminous azure sky stretched and expanded into empty spaces.

Everything here had been sculpted by nature, carved and moulded by the earth, as if directed by the dragons. The cool and distant beauty of the rocks was clouded by mist. It was a work of art, nature's art, touched by the hand of creation across the wide canvas of the world. I could only imagine the view from the sky; birds must see a mesmerizing puzzle of glittering jewels.

I imagined dragons playing in the water of the bay, glimmering in the mist, slithering around the rocks. I wasn't surprised this place wooed and enthralled the mighty creatures. The cliffs and the clear water echoed an ancient time, shifted from a fantasyland into this world, out of enchantment and into reality. It seemed like no other place in Vietnam I had visited before. Maybe there was no other place like this on earth.

Endless islands emerged from the misty water. As the boat moved forward, another rock formation would arise, then another, then another. The veil of mists at Hạ Long Bay was enchanting. The essence of Vietnam was infused in these rocks that emerged from the endless sea.

The power of the mists spun a cocoon around me. A sense of well-being, of peace deep inside, overcame me. My whole body became lighter than the air around me. I was caught up by the mists, shifting into the spirit land, up past the misty cliffs of this place of enchantment.

The boat sailed closer to the formation of Incense Burner Islet—a massive square-shaped stone that rose out of the water on four pins that were only visible at low tide. There were deep grooves in the stone running diagonally that made me think of slash marks the dragons could have made as they clawed their way out of the depths of the bay to perch upon the rock for sunbathing. Perhaps they also used it for cúnging. It felt right to me to find a symbol of spirituality, the incense holder, in the bay of dragons—the origin story of my ancestors—as I sought answers about my own origins.

* * *

High on the mountain top at Delphi where the eagles met, and low in the bay at Hạ Long where the dragons descended, I have been blessed to bear witness to the beginnings of sacred spaces. Spaces created first by the hand of the universe, after which humans explained the power of these spaces as divine intervention. Otherwise, the spaces may not be grasped or comprehended within the limits of human understanding. Such are the stories we tell ourselves.

Vietnam, where I was born in the city of Sài Gòn. Born into Vietnamese traditions, language, and spiritual practices. How does my birth in that country inform who I am?

"What are you?"

"Ummmm … Canadian."

"No, I mean where are you from?"

I sigh and cast my eyes downward. Here we go again, would any answer be enough? If I am struggling with that question myself, how can I answer anyone else?

"I was born in Vietnam" is my go-to response. The "I was born" part is factual. Vietnam is the country where I was born and the country I left to come to Canada.

But I am equally from the Canadian prairies. How does my journey to Canada define my beginnings? Reborn into Canadian traditions, language, and spiritual practices? What is the impact on a child of immigrants living in the inner city of a prairie town?

To self-identify as belonging to a race—to check a box—oversimplifies the complex and rich nature of cultural background. That sort of identification does not convey the intricacies and nuances I navigate on a daily basis. That sort of identification sets up limits and expectations I do not embrace or internalize. "I'm Vietnamese" does not take into consideration my upbringing in Canada and it does not speak to the influences of other cultures on me. It doesn't fit me.

Travelling to these places, collecting the threads:

What is my origin story?

* * *

At each sacred space, I collected a rock, a physical remembrance of space and time, and these became threads. Beyond my personal experience, I'd also collected threads found in different spaces of the world, in different time periods. I was the raw material, bits and pieces, but without the binding elements to put myself together. I still needed to know if I had collected the right number and the right types of threads. I had embarked on an external journey. I wondered what was next, what other journey lay ahead—the journey I would need to travel to help weave the threads together.

By experiencing sacred spaces firsthand, I'd absorbed the energies of those places and in return I left my energy in those places. I feel connected for eternity to those spaces. Reaching back through history and mythology, I see clearly that seeking has been a universal need since the beginning of the world. I continue to be struck by the power of the parallels. The inter-connections. The same stories over and over again.

What will happen when I pass from this life?

What is my purpose in life?

What is my beginning?

These universal questions are contemplated not just by me. The need to connect to spirit is universal. My senses have been opened to the patterns of this need around the world. And ultimately, my senses have opened to the patterns in my own life. Now I am face to face with myself.

My travels through the sacred inform how I live and compel me to ask these questions of myself. I may ask these questions all my life. These questions may not have answers, but the connection to spirit lies in the questioning.

What is my origin story?

How am I the hero of my life?

What happens at the end?

Three: Gates and Goddesses

I ALWAYS ENVIED THOSE WHO BELIEVED. I envied those who lit incense before a statue of a bodhisattva, those who fell to their knees, prayers on their lips, facing Mecca, and those who danced around a fire at Beltane. I wanted to be blessed with the light of the sacred in my eyes, to be wrapped in the serenity of faith. Má and Ba had not imposed faith on me. Now as I was seeking it myself, I was disappointed to discover that faith did not come easily.

My foundation came from ancestor worship through Vietnamese spirituality. My travels through sacred spaces informed the universal questions I asked myself. After travelling, I felt compelled to move inward and to make sense of my experiences. There were threads missing still. Threads I had missed along the way, those I never saw were there. Gaining perspective after time and distance, I had to turn back and collect them, examine them, reflect on them. I invited a pattern or structure to emerge in my search for faith. As I had always found meaning in mythology, I should not have been surprised that the pattern revealed itself through a beloved mythological figure.

I felt like the ancient Sumerian goddess Inanna, standing at the entrance to the netherworld, seeking a way in.

Inanna dwelled above the clouds as the Queen of Heaven. She was the goddess of love, fertility, sex, and war. She wielded power in her own right. She had a fierce and independent feminine power I sought to embody, bold and brave as she stood at the threshold of the unknown.

Inanna married Dumuzi to ensure fertility and prosperity of the land. She also had multiple sexual partners, confident in her desirability, so she became enraged when the hero-god Gilgamesh rejected her. How dare he scorn a queen! He would pay for his disrespect. She sent Gugalanna, the

Bull of Heaven who was the husband of her sister Ereshkigal, Queen of the Dead, to destroy the hero-god. Instead, Gilgamesh and his friend slayed the Bull and hung him in the night sky as a constellation.

Inanna then descended into the underworld to visit her sister Ereshkigal and to attend the funeral of Gugalanna.

Standing at the entrance to the netherworld, adorned with the crown of heaven upon her head, rods of lapis lazuli, necklace, sparkling stones, gold ring, breastplate, and her finest garments, Inanna projected sunbeams radiating from her core. Her dark hair curled around her crown, her chin set, her feet planted, and fire behind her eyes. As Queen of Heaven, she did as she pleased, without care for anyone's judgement. Was she taking a chance leaving her world? What was it worth to her?

> *My lady abandoned heaven, abandoned earth,*
> *To the nether world she descended,*
> *Inanna abandoned heaven, abandoned earth,*
> *To the nether world she descended,*
> *Abandoned lordship, abandoned ladyship,*
> *To the nether world she descended.*

I was like Inanna, standing at the edge of another state of being, another level of understanding, seeking entrance. I attempted to channel the courage of the goddess for the journey ahead.

The underworld was guarded by seven walls, each with a gate. Neti, the gatekeeper, opened each gate to Inanna. He warned her she must abide by the custom and remove a part of her clothing at each gate. Each piece of clothing represented an earthly attribute. In removing each piece, she gave up emblems of her power.

As I mirrored her journey, I too removed something of myself at each gate, the price of entry part of the descent into the otherworld. I had concepts and ideas and expectations of what faith was supposed to be or supposed to do for me. Where and how one should worship, for instance. While I was still only bits and pieces of raw material, some of my fabric needed to be unravelled, the threads cut and thrown away. I needed to toss aside the fabric that no longer served me. Along the path in search of what I sought, I, like Inanna, would give up aspects of my own identity.

First Gate

> *Upon her entering the first gate,*
> *The shugurra, the "crown of the plain" of her head, was removed.*
> *"What, pray, is this?"*
> *"Extraordinarily, O Inanna, have the decrees of*
> *   The nether world been perfected,*
> *O Inanna, do not question the rites of the nether world."*

From age nine to twelve, every Saturday afternoon was spent in Vietnamese school in the frigid basement of Chùa Hải Hội, Winnipeg's only Vietnamese Buddhist Temple. Despite reciting long sentences and recopying dreary passages two hours out of the week, I never learned how to write or read Vietnamese, even though I could speak it. My uncle drove me and my cousins out of the West End over the Arlington Bridge, up above the railway cars, and on the descent, we were greeted by the white "North End" letters on the sloped roof of a house. This was the only time we went to the North End; the neighbourhood could have been a separate country. The chùa was a two-storey building on Burrows Avenue that reminded me of a converted school, set among houses, stone steps leading up to double doors. We left our shoes just inside the entrance, where the ever-present scent of nhang, a specific type of Vietnamese incense, made me gasp and lingered in my hair and on my skin for hours afterwards.

At break time, while my two cousins were drawing pictures of Ninja Turtles, I snuck upstairs to the worship area to spy on the faithful. These weekly peeks at Vietnamese school felt like sinful indulgences. Statues of golden Buddhas floated on lotus blossoms. Against one wall, three statues stood, halos glowing neon behind their heads powered by electricity. I spied on the devoted as they stood before the Buddhas, lit incense, prayed, bowed, and departed. Their backs seemed straighter, and their steps lighter after the ritual.

And around the perimeter of the large main room—behind glass—scenes depicted the Buddha's life, but they were so high on the walls I always had to stand on tippy toes to see them. A brown baby with a smiling couple, the mother wearing what I later knew to be a sari. Next, a boy laughing, dripping gold bangles and ebony locks. Next, a young man turning to leave a sleeping woman and baby. Next, a man sitting under a tree, embraced by leaves, his rib cage visible through stretched skin. And lastly, a man, with long earlobes, eyes closed and palms open, sitting cross-legged on a lotus flower. A halo encircled his head, loose saffron-coloured robes covered his form, and many people surrounded him.

None of the nuns and monks talked to me about Siddhartha Gautama's origins or anything else about Buddhism. I never asked. I only had the pictures. This was before the era of Googling and Siri.

I observed but did not know how to join in. One boy from my Vietnamese class had the chance to beat the gong during break time. His father stood behind him tapping out the rhythm for his son, both with heads down. I looked away, feeling like I was peeking in on a private moment, the two so joined in faith.

Má might have called herself a Buddhist, since she was neither Catholic nor a follower of Cao Đài, another religion popular in Vietnam. Yet she was not a practising Buddhist. She cúnged directly to our ancestors, a tradition embedded in Vietnam long before institutional religions established themselves.

When we did engage in institutional religious practice, we followed Buddhist tradition. At Tết, we went to chùa and picked fortunes for the new year. I sat sandwiched between Má and Jen. Hypnotized by the yellow-clad monks, my heart began beating to the rhythm of their words. I sat with my eyes fixated on all the mandarin oranges glistening under the fluorescent lights, crimson paper taped on their waxy peels, stabbed with the hooks one uses to hang Christmas decorations, fastened to brittle brown branches.

Buddhism had always been there, a part of my background, a part of my heritage. Yet I imagined true faith would be more comparable to true love—a foundation of trust, intense curiosity, fast-fuel passion and slow-burning adoration. Buddhism was my starting point for the sacred, but I couldn't stay there. Buddhism was not my true love.

I deserved to fall in love with my faith.

My unravelling began, as threads loosened and frayed along seams and edges, the fabric that no longer served me slowly falling away. I never prayed or lit incense at chùa. I did not consider myself a Buddhist.

At the first gate, I removed the religion of my birth.

Second Gate

> *Upon her entering the second gate,*
> *The rods of lapis lazuli were removed.*
> *"What, pray, is this?"*
> *"Extraordinarily, O Inanna, have the decrees of*
> *The nether world been perfected,*
> *O Inanna, do not question the rites of the nether world."*

Saturday afternoons after Vietnamese school finished, I was finally able to shut my bedroom door and resume reading my latest book. I curled deep into my bed and hugged it tight. Má was strict so outside of school and swimming, I was not permitted to "loiter" outside the house, even after reaching the age of majority. Being a single parent, she held the reins tight, always with a careful eye on Jen and me so we would grow up to be "good girls." I did not feel chafed. Outside my house, the world was full of strangers and was unpredictable. I wanted to be alone and read. At home, I was free to walk in the worlds of my imaginings.

Through my books, I travelled with many others, besides Inanna, to the underworld. In Greek mythology, I walked with Orpheus as he led his love Eurydice back to the land of the living, forbidden to look behind him to see if she followed; my heart broke when he cast a quick glance and lost her all over again. In Egyptian mythology, I also attended the judgement ceremony, the deceased person's heart was placed on the scale and weighed against the feather of Maat. The deceased stood before Osiris, Lord of the

Underworld, after being led there by jackal-headed Anubis, who clutched the ankh, the symbol of life, in his hand.

Myth had always been my first love and when I landed my first job the summer between high school and university, I had more means and opportunity to indulge it. I became a bookseller at Smithbooks at Polo Park Shopping Centre. Thanks to my employee discount, I dropped a large chunk of my hourly wages adding to my personal collection. Books of mythology, folklore, fairy tales, and mysterious places I rescued from the store bookshelves and adopted.

Throughout university, although I was a business school student, all my electives were in creative writing, religion, and feminist studies. I found myself sneaking away from Organizational Theory and Management Information Systems to embrace Advanced Creative Writing and Storytelling. I walked briskly away from the Drake Centre of the Asper School of Business, left classmates with their calculators, day planners, highlighters, huddled together in endless group work. I floated on light feet to the Tier Building and greeted Arts students clutching coil-bound notebooks, novels with neon post-it flags sticking out, to discuss themes and theories.

Through my electives, archaeologist Marija Gimbutas and cultural historian Riane Eisler introduced me to the divine feminine—the worship of the Great Goddess. Controversy swirled around the discovery of ancient matriarchal societies. Was there historical evidence to support their existence, or were they conceptualized to enhance the work of the second wave of feminism? That wasn't what mattered to me. The Goddess mattered.

I knew of different goddesses and gods from world mythologies, but they were not God—the omnipresent being. It had never occurred to me before that the ever-present one could be anything other than male, could be anything other than God.

This revelation began to weave together with my emerging feminism. Who benefited from perpetuating the construct of the divine as male? Male as closest to holy. Female as embodiment of temptation, side characters but never the protagonist. Growing up, I did not see myself represented in the prevalent idea of God as an old bearded white man, in a long robe and sandals. He/him. Somehow I had accepted it as the image of the divine, even though it did not resonate with me.

GODDESS resonated. GODDESS vibrated in my mind.

Through my lens of mythology, I gave myself permission to be represented and reflected in great goddesses from around the world—Athena, Kali, Isis—powerful goddesses of wisdom, of change, of love, and ultimately of feminine value. The divine feminine became the framework in my quest to discover the light of the sacred.

This was an important redefinition of spirituality for me. It shifted my perspective, my lens of the divine.

I removed my male-centric concepts of faith.

Third Gate

Upon her entering the third gate,
The small lapis lazuli stones of her neck were removed.
"What, pray, is this?"
"Extraordinarily, O Inanna, have the decrees of
The nether world been perfected,
O Inanna, do not question the rites of the nether world."

Má had one piece of jewellery she wore consistently. Hanging on a simple yellow gold chain, the pendant was an oval the size of a quarter. A willowy woman stood within it, almost windblown, moulded into the shimmering glass, which was encircled by a thin border of yellow gold. Quan Âm.

Even though I always had questions about faith, I had never thought to ask Má about the significance of her necklace. So I did what I learned to do in university—I studied it myself. I wrote a paper for my World Religions class.

Known more formally as Quán Thế Âm Bồ Tát, she is the Buddhist bodhisattva of compassion. A bodhisattva is someone who has broken the cycle of life and death and has achieved nirvana—enlightenment—the ultimate goal in Buddhism. Instead of entering that realm, however, she remains on earth to help others reach enlightenment. The bodhisattva of compassion originated in India as Avolokitshvara, a male entity. As Buddhism spread from India to China in the 3rd century A.D. and then to Vietnam, Avolokitshvara merged with local female deities, and their qualities, to emerge as a powerful female figure. She is Kuan Yin to the Chinese. She is Kannon to the Japanese. She is beyond Buddhism, she is a goddess. Quan Âm—she who hears the cries of the world.

Years later, on a family trip to Vietnam (Ryan's first), the year I turned twenty-seven, we travelled to a Buddhist temple along the road home to Trảng Bàng. Some of my aunts lit incense and bowed. One aunt, Cô Tám, was not a believer, and stood on the side. She never entered a temple or engaged in any of the rituals. I stood with her on the outside.

Quan Âm met me in front of the temple, a statue elevated above the earth on a stone platform. She was glorious, carved from white marble with delicate grey veins flowing throughout her body. She was standing on a blooming lotus flower, one hand slanted in front of her body and the other hand pouring the elixir of life into the earth.

Her eyes were closed. A holiness swirled around her, as perceptible as the incense from the incense burner below.

Ryan and I were newlyweds, so I was both nervous and excited to show him the land of my ancestors with which I had such a complicated relationship. I tried to imagine what it was like through his eyes. His first time in Asia. This was the first time he had ever seen a Buddhist temple. With his pale skin and hazel eyes, he was the visible minority here. At 5'10", Ryan was not considered tall in Canada, but he towered over most people here. Everywhere we went, I was stared at, passers-by whispering Việt Kiều—overseas Vietnamese, and he was stared at, người tây—Western person. Curiosities.

Ryan took our picture. In the photo, I stand in front of Quan Âm, the top of my head reaching the lotus flower upon which she stands, the orange and pink and white daisies on my sleeveless shirt suggesting a bouquet offering for the great lady at her feet. My head was in the path of the elixir of life flowing from her vessel.

Once my eyes had been opened to the divine feminine in my university studies, I could and would see the goddess everywhere. Whereas before, she might have surrounded me, but I never noticed her. Now I could not stop myself from seeing her. This phenomenon is common from what I recall from my introductory psychology class. My eyes were open to much more now, such as privilege and patriarchy.

I had seen Quan Âm in the homes of family friends in Winnipeg and perhaps she'd been one of the statues at the chùa on Burrows Avenue.

I had seen statues of Quan Âm on previous trips to Vietnam as a kid and as a teenager, part of the landscape, as ubiquitous as rice fields and motorbikes.

Travelling in Vietnam on this trip, I found her presence pervasive, on every home altar, in every temple and every taxicab. Here, she was not just spirit and air, she was life and love.

She was the goddess I had known the longest, the goddess from the country of my birth. She had always been there, patient and unobtrusive, waiting for me to notice and acknowledge her. While Buddhism was background noise I chose to mute, Quan Âm became background noise I chose to enhance and amplify. I was looking forward to getting to know her better, bringing her light into my life. I had no need for a priest or a monk, I could connect with Quan Âm directly, like I could with the spirits of my ancestors. My unravelling continued as more threads loosened.

I removed the notion that spirituality was all-or-nothing.

Fourth Gate

> Upon her entering the fourth gate,
> The sparkling stones of her breast were removed.
> "What, pray, is this?"
> "Extraordinarily, O Inanna, have the decrees of
>   The nether world been perfected,
> O Inanna, do not question the rites of the nether world."

The year after our trip to Vietnam, Ryan and I had travelled to Egypt when I was twenty-eight. We visited the Valley of the Kings, a mountain range on the west bank of the Nile, where the great pharaohs were laid to eternal rest, hidden within the valley generations after pyramid-building ended.

White and dusty limestone shimmered against the desert sunlight. A few of the tombs were open to tourists including the tomb of Ramses VI—KV9.

After I passed through the iron gate at the entrance, I was transported back to the Egyptian underworld. I was encircled by elaborate hieroglyphics on both walls as we descended through the long tunnel leading to the room that once housed Pharaoh. Hieroglyphics depicted scenes from the Book of the Dead—gods with animal heads and thousands of people escorting Pharaoh on his journey.

Standing beside the sarcophagus, I looked up at the ceiling to see one of the most famous scenes in the entire Valley: giant Nut, heavenly mother in two mirror images, one on each half of the ceiling.

When Nut, goddess of the sky, had married her twin brother Geb, their union angered the sun god Ra. He punished them by having Shu, the god of air, separate them for all eternity. Nut became the sky above and Geb became the earth below. Nut reached for her beloved, vaulting across the heavens, but could only balance on her outstretched fingers and toes, which became the four points creating the cardinal directions.

On one half of the tomb ceiling, Nut arched above me, her head and arms pushing up from the bottom of one wall, her body stretching up to the ceiling and across and extending down along the opposite wall, her feet pointing in the direction of the floor, in an impossibly long downward-facing dog yoga pose. She was black-haired. Her naked yellow skin was dotted with golden stars, embodying the entire heavenly realm, with red swollen suns shown against her starry body. Nut was the mother to all gods, swallowing the sun god in the evening to give birth to him in the morning.

I smiled at Ryan. On this trip, we celebrated our third wedding anniversary. It meant so much to me to be here in Egypt, and to be able to share it with him.

I had been in love with Egyptian mythology since I was in junior high, reading books late into the night in my tiny room in Winnipeg's West End. The goddesses and gods glided into my dreams.

Standing in Nut's heavenly embrace, a tingling sensation, warm and weighty, poured over me from the top of my head, around my shoulders, down my back, and down my legs and through the tips of my toes, then into the earth, feelings of wellness and hope. As I gazed at Nut's golden body created many generations ago, from one end of the ceiling to the other, back and forth, it felt like the ceiling had dropped down to just above my head; it was a dizzying effect, like being caught up in a spell. Her role was protectress, between chaos and order, to shelter all in her realm, and to guard against the unknown beyond cosmic space. The sky shrank to envelop me alone and Nut herself wrapped her starry arms around me.

A member of our tour group coughed, and the spell was broken. I tried to hold on to that feeling. Although it was like trying to grasp incense with my fingers or like trying to clasp a ray of sunlight to my chest, I cherished the feeling.

I removed the distance between myself and the divine.

Fifth Gate

> Upon her entering the fifth gate,
> The gold ring of her hand was removed.
> "What, pray, is this?"
> "Extraordinarily, O Inanna, have the decrees of
>   The nether world been perfected,
> O Inanna, do not question the rites of the nether world."

Waking up to my alarm, I pressed snooze, easing out of my dream of bathing in shimmering gold lakes and falling through dark space, before rolling out of bed for the day, checking as I did a hundred times a day, my growing belly, round and firm.

Eight minutes until the bus, I hurried to put on my jewellery. My wedding band and my engagement ring were starting to feel snug. I fastened the necklace I had been wearing every day for the last month—a figure of a naked woman with arms stretched wide over her head, no discernable face, naked breasts, a spiral at her abdomen, and legs closed together. The pendant reminded me of Venus figurines discovered all over Europe, dating back to the Paleolithic period. These statuettes made from such material as stone, bone, and clay all share similar characteristics of heavy breasts, full abdomens, wide hips, thighs, and buttocks, tapered at the head and at the legs. Some of the figures suggest pregnancy.

Walking to the bus stop, I put my hands into the pockets of my jacket, although it was not chilly, as spring was ushering in summer, signs of tiny buds on the trees and shy blades of grass. I again spread my fingers over my growing tummy and involuntarily smiled. In my second trimester of my first pregnancy, I was conscious of my body in a way I had never been before. I weighed myself constantly. I took my pre-natal vitamins. I followed all the guidelines for what not to consume. I practised yoga and used the treadmill at the Y downtown. I felt conscious of the control I had over my body—what I did could have lasting effects on the fetus, my "Fety," and at the same time I felt conscious of the lack of control I had—my body was growing a human life without my direct work. I needed to embrace the fact that my body would do as it willed and my job was to provide it with the proper conditions and input. Fety took what was needed. I watched and waited for signs of pregnancy and was thrilled when symptoms manifested, each symptom affirming that life had taken root deep inside my womb and sprouted.

On the bus, I plopped into a side seat above the back wheel. Sometimes sitting on a side seat made me nauseous, so instead of reading, I closed my eyes. I touched the pendant, cool between my fingers before it warmed to my touch. Jen had bought it for me when we were travelling in England together the previous month. Me, her, and Fety. After gazing through the veil to Avalon on the Tor and visiting the grave-site of King Arthur, we had walked around the town. Glastonbury was a New Age haven. Wiccans and pagans embraced the land. The Great Goddess and the Green Man ruled there together. Boutique shops filled with healing crystals, incense, jewellery, and symbols, surrounded us.

I had wanted a piece of that enchanted land, a piece to bring back home. In one of the shops, I'd been naturally drawn to the silver pendant.

As I was rocked by the moving bus on my way to work, I rubbed the grooves of the spiral between my fingers, lost in the motion. This piece of the Goddess I had brought back into my Winnipeg life, that I could hold in my hands, was also an amulet I could wear around my neck everyday. The spiral represented energy outward to the external world and energy inward to the spiritual core at the same time. This symbol, often used by Wiccans, signified life. The spiral represented the cycle of life, death, and rebirth. Spirals in general are found in nature and in art. The spiral also represented creation, the womb, and the beautiful light of motherhood.

I had always envied those who announced to the world their faith. I had always envied those who wore around their necks the Cross, the Star of David, the Om, the Buddha. To express faith with talismans or clothing or anything outside oneself required both bravery and vulnerability. I felt more fabric that no longer served me fall away.

I removed my discomfort with outward spiritual expression.

Sixth Gate

> *Upon her entering the sixth gate,*
> *The breastplate of her breasts were removed.*
> *"What, pray, is this?"*
> *"Extraordinarily, O Inanna, have the decrees of*
> *   The nether world been perfected,*
> *O Inanna, do not question the rites of the nether world."*

Being pregnant, I was even more conscious of everything about my body, from my diet, to exercise, and the way I walked, to how my mind worked. My thoughts and emotions may have an effect on Fety, according to the pregnancy websites. Although I'd practised it for years, yoga meant something different now to me. I made a conscious effort to regulate and be mindful of my thoughts, to bring awareness to what I intended, and yoga became a more valuable endeavour for mindfulness.

Energy flow is an essential part of yoga and had always been part of my yoga practice. Breathe in and breathe out. Energy flowed through me as I moved through a vinyasa—a series of movements to transition from one asana to another. Starting in standing position, bending over, hands on the mat, stepping back to plank pose, exhaling to low plank, inhaling to upward facing dog, and exhaling to downward-facing dog, jumping forward. I often felt the yogic fire deep inside myself. The internal heat from this series burned for a long period of time, strengthening my body. Yoga appealed to me as a physical challenge, a path through which to build strength and flexibility, stretch my muscles, align my spine, and reach for the soles of my feet. I reveled in the mental conditioning it took to hold tree pose for a moment longer than when I thought I would lose my balance and step out of the pose. The sense of achievement was thrilling after completing an entire class of Bikram yoga, accomplishing all twenty-six poses in the humidity of the studio, embracing the discomfort, dizziness and weakness on the edge of my senses, being able to push through it and find the strength to do one more pose, and one more pose after that, and one more pose after that.

When it was time to meditate at the end of class, lying in savasana, corpse pose, my yoga instructor reminded me to bring my awareness to different areas in my body. Relax your toes. Your toes are relaxed. Relax your hips. Your hips are relaxed. Before my pregnancy, my mind wandered to grocery-list making, what I would have for lunch after class, and the book I was reading, and I let my mind go there.

Only once I was pregnant was I motivated to expand my focus beyond the physical realm. Only once I was pregnant did I challenge myself with conscious breathing. I wanted to do it for Fety.

Moving into utkata konasana, goddess pose, I stood sideways on my mat with my legs wide apart. Turned my feet out towards the corners, knees in line over the ankles. Slowly bent my knees, making sure they were still over the ankles, and lowered into a squat, keeping my spine straight, imagining a string pulling me up from the top of my head. Moved my arms into prayer pose, heart centre, pushing my palms together and pulling my elbows apart. In week 35 of my pregnancy, my bump was heavy, pulled down by gravity, pushed up by my frame. This pose worked my pelvic floor and opened my hips for labour, hopefully only a few weeks away.

I concentrated on my breathing. To consciously breathe, I gave myself over to the moment. There was only the moment. Focus and bring the mind back to the breath from where it wandered. There was only the breath. My breathing was the only thing within my control. Focusing on my breathing soothed the fears and doubts of impending motherhood, and brought calm and optimism. I felt energy flowing to my womb like shimmering liquid gold as it travelled from my heart, through my blood vessels, to nourish the one inside me. There was no past and no future, only that moment. The only thing that existed at that moment was the exhale, the space in between, and the inhale.

I found joy in the space in between the exhale and the inhale, a time of suspension, of holding, of waiting. While my body did the work of growing a human, I was waiting for the arrival. The gentle fluttering in my belly evolved into sharp jabs and swift kicks as bones hardened. It was a delicious feeling, intense and prickly at the back of my spine. I feared the uncertainty and the pain of labour. I was nervous about what my life would be like with a baby.

Waiting for my daughter to detach from my body, to become her own person, from fetus to infant, I glowed from anticipation. Soon she would take her first breath, independently of me. She would be herself and I would be myself, two separate entities. I envisioned a little baby, her breathing alongside mine.

As I held the pose, I channeled the goddess, the shimmering liquid gold flowing through both our bodies. Sometimes Quan Âm. Sometimes Nut. Glimpses of Inanna. A sacred dance of body and mind and spirit, to create something that had never been before.

My unravelling was continuing, the seams busted and the loose threads dangling.

I removed the notion that spiritual practice could not be integrated into ordinary experiences.

Seventh Gate

> Upon her entering the seventh gate,
> All the garments of ladyship of her body were removed.
> "What, pray, is this?"
> "Extraordinarily, O Inanna, have the decrees of
>   The nether world been perfected,
> O Inanna, do not question the rites of the nether world."

My eagerness for the anticipated amazement of motherhood quickly dissolved after the birth of my daughter Lexi. Life became measured in three-
hour increments—feed her, encourage her with appropriate stimuli and
bonding, then help her find sleep. Only to be repeated. I should sleep when
the baby sleeps, said all the guidebooks and helpful blogs. Yet both adren-
aline and loneliness prevented my slumber; how could I sleep knowing I
would have to feed her again in 45 minutes? I missed Ryan, at work during
the day, and when he came home, I tried to nap, preparing for the long night
ahead. It was a completely surprising state. Nothing had prepared this new
mother for the isolation delivered alongside the "bundle of joy."

Whenever Lexi refused to breastfeed, I handed her to Ryan and went
into the bathroom and sobbed. And when she cried, she turned red-faced
and seemed to stop breathing, while my arms trembled under her weight.
In my sleep-deprived fog, I felt isolated and insecure, highly sensitive and
strangely detached. When I fed her at three a.m., the deepest part of night,
Ryan snoring in the other room, it felt like my daughter and I were the only
two beings in the whole world.

My daughter was the sun, radiating life and light, and I revolved around
her. We were pulled to each other by invisible forces, her need to feed, or
pushed together, her need to be held constantly. I wrapped her in blue fabric
and strapped her to my body, her chest to my chest, her head cradled just
under my neck, her cheek resting on my collarbone, her eyelashes fluttering
against my skin. Glued together, we were one, not two, fused.

After I became a mother, I lost myself, and also lost my way on my path.
I felt lost in the ordinary. I was no longer contemplating great goddesses,
or sensing Quan Âm beside me, or feeling Nut above me, and the spiral
goddess was tucked away in my jewellery box. I was not binding myself
together with the threads I had collected. I was just concentrating on day-
to-day life and did not know how to integrate my spiritual search during
those early days of new motherhood.

Then Lexi turned fourteen months old and I was putting her down for
her afternoon nap on an ordinary Monday afternoon in January. I had gone
back to work part-time and the previous week at work had been filled with

emotional landmines. Ryan was working overtime every day. It was the coldest week in Winnipeg in two years. I needed Lexi to sleep so I could do the housecleaning I'd planned. I cuddled her in my arms in the rocking chair, singing "Hush Little Baby." Her head was on my chest, her hot breath against my breast. At the end of the song, she sat up and looked at me. Her room was mostly dark, sunlight peeking around the edges of the black-out blinds.

My beautiful baby girl looked at me. Her eyes were deep pools of awareness.

I see you. I know you.

Energy built up within me and ran through my whole body, flowing outward.

Her eyes were soulful eyes. She was the spirit of my spirit. Then everything became so vivid, the outside world sharper, energy flowing inward.

In that moment, I saw the goddess behind my daughter's eyes. I saw the sacred in her. I hugged her close to me and kissed the top of her head, inhaling her familiar baby scent.

"Lex, I love you," I whispered.

She was silent.

We rocked together in unison. She fell asleep.

I had given birth to her and my breast milk alone had nourished her for her first six months. She was my personal sacred. A thread connected her to Má through me and beyond this life, to Bà Ngoại, all the way back to the Trưng sisters. The ancestors were near, shimmering in the shadows of dark corners, slipping in and out of air.

My body tingled from the top of my head, through to my toes, glittering gold flowing through me as life force. My spirit suddenly overflowed with emotion, with awareness. I became aware of a deep hum at the base of my navel, the centre, vibrating, listening to it, feeling it.

In my mind's eye, my collected threads wove themselves together: Quan Âm, the spiral goddess, the divine feminine, spirit. Energy and power radiated outwards and inwards. Only the present moment existed.

I removed the notion that spiritual experience needed to be grand, that it could not exist in the quiet moments.

The Return

After passing all seven gates, Inanna stood naked before the judges of the nether world.

> At their word, the word which tortures the spirit,
> The sick woman was turned into a corpse,
> The corpse was hung from a stake.

No one returned to the land of the living after descending into the underworld.

Like Inanna, I was stripped bare at the deepest level, removed of that which made up my spiritual self. Faith wasn't what I thought it to be. I had not realized I'd built a box around myself that became the limitations and barriers to my sacred quest. I unravelled and dismantled my misconceptions of spirit.

These were the trappings of my former self. I sacrificed my previous self—the "me" before motherhood and my spiritual awakening—at the altar of my emerging self. The "me" I was would never be again. I mourned my familiar former self to become my new self, someone changed and wholly unknown.

I already had my foundation of Vietnamese spirituality. I already had threads I had found along my travels through sacred spaces.

Now I threw away fragments of myself that were no longer serving me. I cut away the threads that were binding me, holding me back, that had not allowed me to move forward. I no longer felt like just bits and pieces of raw material that did not fit together. I had found the ethereal framework in which to weave together the pieces of my spirit.

Now that I was bare, I could begin to re-stitch myself with the knowledge I had gained passing through each gate. I was spiritual, not religious. The divine was all around me and I could weave together my own faith. I could express and practise my own spirituality.

Inanna's handmaiden, the goddess Ninshubur, mourned for her and sought help from the gods. The god Enki fashioned two beings who travelled to the netherworld and sprinkled food and water on Inanna's body.

Inanna ascends from the nether world,
The Anunnaki fled,
And whoever of the nether world may have descended
peacefully to the nether world;
When Inanna ascends from the nether world,
Verily the dead hasten ahead of her.

Like Inanna's faithful servant, my daughter became my companion, who called me back to the light.

I had what I needed to fashion myself anew. With this new-found understanding, I felt ready to face the world. I would be able to deal with whatever came my way in my life. I would be able to face any monster, fight any battle, and weather any storm.

I ascended from the nether world. The emergence of a spiritual seeker. The light of the sacred flickered within me.

A crack in the window, a doorway not quite shut, a lid slightly ajar.
Enough of an opening through which
light may pass,
air may flow,
water may seep,
and spirit may come.

PART II
SPIRIT EXPERIENCED

Four: Out of Egypt

THE FIRST NIGHT I EVER SPENT away from my daughter, I stared at a picture of Lexi that Ryan texted me as he was getting her ready for bed. Mini hoop earrings in her newly pierced ears (a Vietnamese tradition) peeked out of her dark hair. All I wanted to feel under my fingers was the soft fleece of her bunny pyjamas. All I wanted to do was reach out and caress her chubby cheeks and inhale deeply her sweet milky breath.

I was visiting a different office of the Workplace than the one I worked at. Staying at a motel where I checked in at the attached restaurant, I laid a thread-bare towel on the bed, questioning the cleanliness of the flowery bedspread. I then emptied the contents of my laptop bag to take inventory once again for the next day. My business cards. Copies of the employee assistance program brochure. Letter-sized lined notepads, pens, highlighters, post-it notes, Kleenex, more Kleenex. I packed everything up again, breathing in short breaths, my fingers numb.

I hung up my outfit for the next day, dark grey pants, black sleeveless blouse with small red and orange flowers, and a black cardigan. Short black boots with a slight heel. Picking out my outfit had taken a lot of time; I needed the right look to convey both professionalism and empathy. I was there to support employees who were being let go.

I also felt my invisible garment, warming my skin, light as air and hard as armour, still wrapped around me. This garment was fashioned from the threads I had collected throughout my travels and woven together through self-reflection and self-care.

What a difference a week made. Going back to work part-time had made the time I spent with Lexi make sense, gave it purpose. Last week on my day off, I felt the power of spirit flow through me as I was putting Lexi down for a nap. I was like Inanna transformed. That felt like the real moment, of life and faith, and living in the light. Today made up the otherworld, a land of deadlines, deliverables, teleconferences, work I was paid to perform. The wind howled outside, whipping the snow around, tugging it this way only to blow it that way. The deep prairie chill of January. The temperature was so low that the consistency of the snow was not tacky, ready for snowperson building, but was instead fine powder, grains repelling each other. The wind, not a lullaby, was instead an alert.

I lay there between sheets that smelled of bleach. I took in a deep breath. After natural delivery and a year of maternity leave, anything was doable … wasn't it? I kept telling myself—I could do this.

While I was on mat leave, the Workplace had undergone its own journey of transformation, bringing about organizational change and a shift in corporate culture. The Workplace needed to modernize its business practices in response to the changing needs of clients and to remain relevant in the new economic reality, said the official Workplace communications. What did it really mean? A reduction in its workforce. My Leader, who'd hired me and mentored me, had retired, like my Leader's Leader who'd hugged me when I came to work for the Workplace. Would I be alone now?

I slept shallowly, listening for my baby during the night, and woke up in darkness, afraid I would sleep through my alarm. Once the alarm finally went off, I dressed quickly and put on my jewellery, first my white gold hoops and white gold engagement ring reunited with my wedding band. Then I added my white gold necklace of Quan Âm, the one I'd purchased in Vietnam a few years earlier. The pendant the size of a dime depicts the goddess seated cross-legged on a lotus, palms together in prayer pose, halo around her.

Everyday while pregnant with Lexi, I had worn the pendant of the spiral goddess that I brought back from Glastonbury, England, on my trip with Jen. It had felt like a talisman for sacred motherhood. After Lexi, I set that pendant aside, almost like it had completed its magic, fulfilled its purpose. Representations of the divine feminine such as Egyptian Nut and Sumerian Inanna also felt far away. Yet, there was something about Quan Âm that still resonated with me. She was the goddess I had known the longest, the goddess from the country of my birth. I wanted to see a representation of myself in her. I still envied the yellow gold-plated pendant of the goddess Má wore and cherished. My white gold pendant of Quan Âm had hung in my jewellery box for years, worn only a handful of times, as if it was waiting for me. The goddess of mercy is also commonly portrayed as a woman with a thousand eyes to see the suffering in the world and a thousand arms outstretched to help those in need. I sought a connection to Quan Âm. I had begun actively seeking a relationship with her, above any other goddess. She became the focal point for my tentative weaving together of faith.

Quan Âm embodies a gentle power. The power of compassion, the act of mercy, the desire to be of service to others. I wanted to invite more of those virtues into my life. I did not want to be so consumed by my own immediate concerns but to move toward being less self-centred. Who didn't? Motherhood made me want to cultivate patience and compassion, qualities I may not have focussed on before they became so relevant and necessary to me as a new mother. Like the stories of heroes King Arthur and Emperor Lê had revealed to me ways to be a hero in my own life, Quan Âm represented powers I was striving to embody.

Merciful Lady, show me your light. Let it shine through me to the people who will need it. The weight of the pendant anchored me to the present as the sharp coolness of the metal warmed to my body temperature.

I grasped Quan Âm between my fingers. After working for the Workplace for twelve years, today was the first time I had visited this satellite office. I'd spent many years conducting interviews, giving advice and guidance to managers regarding performance issues, organizing training sessions. There were so many roles to be played in Human Resources. Supporting employees through work transition was the most challenging. I didn't realize it then that in the coming months, I would pay a high price, giving more of myself than I expected. The Dark Days cast their shadow across my path that frigid winter day as I made my own exodus.

* * *

Shortly before I went on maternity leave with Lexi, I was asked by my old Leader to write an article for the Workplace's regional newsletter regarding change and transition ("to help people," in his words). While most organizational change focusses on leaders—those with the responsibility and accountability to authorize decisions—and how to lead change, I wondered what change meant for an employee? Since the span of control and the span of influence for an employee is much smaller, the employee became the emphasis of my article. What was the cost to the employee, in terms of mental and emotional health, of navigating through change? What effect did this have on the spirit of the employee?

My piece summarized the Bridges Transition Model in which William Bridges discusses Moses and the Exodus as an allegory of organizational transformation. I was surprised to discover that my journey through work over the next little while would mirror this model's three phases so closely.

- Endings—The person must leave Egypt behind and leave their old identity. After crossing the Red Sea, there is no turning back.
- The Neutral Zone—The person wanders the wilderness, the old identity fading away. The person is between what once was and what is yet to become.
- New Beginnings—The person reaches the promised land, altered by the experience, creating a new identity.
- I would come to internalize:
- Change is external. Change is situational. Change may be fast.
- Transition is internal. Transition is psychological. Transition may be slow.

* * *

After visiting the other office, I returned home to Ryan and Lexi and my regular life and tried to wrap their arms around me, a cocoon against the uneasiness at work. I ran my fingers along my daughter's smooth cheek after our first-ever overnight separation. I hugged Má as she welcomed me home and ladled out noodle soup for me, Ryan, and Lexi. My invisible garment began to feel heavy on my shoulders, the threads straining at the seams. It was dark when I went to work, and it was dark when I left work. The sky was tinted orange ushering in dawn, but the sparkling ice crystals and blue hue faded to black at sunset. I bundled up in my down-filled parka, water-proof boots, Quan Âm around my neck, and my earbuds playing meditation podcasts, warding off the deep snow and high wind chill factors. Spring was still far off in the imagination.

Sitting at my workstation, I reviewed my growing to-do list in my pink coil-bound notebook. I wrote emails to my work address when I was in bed at night, mind clutter chasing away sleep, and transcribed the tasks in my binder the next morning. It used to be such a thrill, to be able to check off items. It meant that I was helpful in some way to someone. Now, my to-do list was the sobering embodiment of all the consequences that came along with transformation. I often rubbed my egg-shaped worry rock, the one I got in university when I volunteered as a student peer advisor, the stone becoming smooth and polished, the shade of graphite with thin white veins.

I printed off updated organizational charts every month or so. When I looked at the one for Human Resources, there I was, a number in a rect-angular box. But my box didn't report to the box it had reported to two months ago. I blinked, looked again, and felt pin pricks in my fingers and heat at the back of my neck.

To someone else, sitting in the Central Office in a different city, this was a paper exercise. This organizational structure made the most sense for the New Workplace. Someone looking at a computer monitor moved the boxes around, deleted some of them, and renamed some of them. Then someone else approved the changes. Efficiency achieved. Task completed. It was decided.

Change is external. Change is situational. Change may be fast.

I had been realigned to fit the new organizational structure.

Transition is internal. Transition is psychological. Transition may be slow.

But I wasn't a box.

I had given my heart to the Workplace for more than ten years. I was doing all I could for employees who were worried about their jobs, giving of myself even now. I was wrapped in familiar garments of past expectations and past accomplishments. This was my beloved Workplace, my work family. But the family was coming undone – some had retired, some had been replaced, while others were still there but were undergoing their own transformations, no longer recognizable to me.

I was a box.

The Workplace had changed. It had become cold and uncommunicative, no longer interested in my needs or my opinions. I didn't realize that until now. The Workplace was about to break up with me. *It's not you, it's me,* if I read between the lines. I could be next. I didn't know what was going to happen next.

I threw the organization chart into the recycling blue bin, wet with my tears. The threads of my invisible garment loosened and began to unravel. I grabbed Quan Âm around my neck and stared at the family portrait on my desk. I still had a lot to do today, employees who needed me, Ryan and Lexi who needed me to do this work. Quan Âm became a barrier, numbing me to ward off the sorrow, a necessary separation to keep going.

* * *

Working for the Workplace began to require more than I was willing to give. How to contemplate spirituality in the evenings and on weekends when I was weighed down by work during the days? Emotional landmines at work drained me. The emotional labour at work increased a little everyday, how long would it be before it became too much to bear? I was giving everything of myself at work to be a support for others. I needed some left for my husband and my daughter, to not let the darkness touch them and our life at home. My goal was to be energetic enough for puzzles with Lexi after dinner, for bath, book, and bedtime, for butterfly kisses and rounds of "Hush Little Baby." The nights always concluded with a sprint to finish tidying the house, running errands, and making lunches for the next day. And falling into bed, exhausted. But then, my eyes flew open as work mind-clutter chased off sleep.

I was giving away the pieces I had fashioned together walking with Inanna. I was giving away pieces of myself at work, pieces I needed for Ryan and Lexi, pieces I needed for the rest of my life. It was the beginning of the end, Moses leading the Israelites out of Egypt, the path ahead unclear.

My best friend kidnapped me on a frosty Saturday evening. "You need to get out," she said. On nights like this one, when the prairies were plunged into blackness and the wind chill threatened to freeze skin in less than a minute, it was too easy to wrap myself up in warm blankets, fuzzy socks, and build a nest against the world. I didn't want to hang out with my best friend or exercise with Jen or go over to Má's for dinner. After laying Lexi in her crib, Ryan and I barely had enough energy to stumble downstairs and collapse on the couch.

I loved musicals and my best friend usually went with the flow, so we went to see the movie *Les Misérables*. In the beginning sequence, the prisoner #24601 Jean Valjean, and his fellow prisoners, toil in the shipyard, and remind themselves to "Look Down."

As the ensemble sang about looking down, not looking them in the eye, being here until you die, tears burst from my eyes—that's what happened, they burst out. A barrier broke. What was supposed to remain contained sprang a leak. Why had we picked this movie? *I'm standing in my grave.* Overdramatic, perhaps, yet there was a little truth to it—I was just a number, just a number in a box.

I tried to swallow my cries until I was making a choking guttural sound in my throat. My best friend turned and put her hand on my arm. I shook my head and gave her a weak smile.

Quan Âm, where are you?

Throughout this time, I had sought out Quan Âm. As the goddess of my ancestors, she became the centre of my search for faith. Yet my chosen goddess became mysterious. Silent. Hard to get to know. Seeking her out, I invited her into my life. I invited in her light. I asked questions of her and pondered when she would appear, a presence in my life.

When I had started as a summer student at the Workplace when I was twenty, after my second year of university, I was so nervous—my first job ever in an office. I was shown to a desk, my own desk, with a computer, and a chair.

"Nice to meet you, Linda," my new co-worker said to me. Her hand was warm and wrinkly grasping mine. "Do you plan on being with the Workplace for a while?"

"I don't know."

"Well, if you stay for five years, you'll be here for life."

Twelves years later, I was still here. My long service plaque was displayed at my workstation, along with family photos, stuffed animals, rocks, and prints from Vietnam.

I'd felt so honoured when I received an offer of full-time employment after university graduation. A steady job. Health care and dental plan. A pension. What Má had always wanted for me. What Ba had probably always wanted for me. This was an immigrant parents' dream. My work in human resources providing advice and guidance to internal clients was challenging and engaging. My colleagues became my work family. They saw me through graduation. My wedding. They threw me a baby shower. We supported each other, held each other up and knew each other well. I talked to them more often in a week than I did to Má or Jen.

My New Leader, after being with us for a month, said to me, "This is not a family. It's a workplace."

∗ ∗ ∗

In the darkness, however, a light sparked. Born from the misery and uncertainty of work. Out of nothing, there was a compulsion for something. I felt the need to generate a little light for myself. A light to illuminate the shadows between the spaces in my life.

As the vernal equinox ushered in a new season, the return of the light, the earth spun towards the longest day of the year. The cycle shifted, breaking the deep freeze, and awakening life that had laid dormant.

Notes scribbled in journals.

Fractured sentences emailed to myself.

Lines typed on my phone while on the bus.

Flashes of insight and knowledge written down, captured in words.

I began writing again.

As a kid, I had jotted down stories and fairy tales in my coil-bound note-book. I wrote for pure pleasure, felt compelled to do so. These imaginings were doorways into other realities and alternate lives that held possibilities, outside my own front door.

Awakening. Emerging. I was entering a new season for myself, where I felt compelled to capture my experiences in a form other than journaling on birthdays and travels. I started focussing on my own stories of my own world and my own life. This was the right time and it was the right material. A tingling within my fingers and a light flickering at my navel confirmed that this was what I enjoyed. My body remembered. My spirit remembered. The lightness and the utter focus.

I looked up literary magazines open for submission. I researched virtual writing courses. I set a goal to apply that fall for the Manitoba Writers' Guild Mentorship Program for the following year. These plans kept me motivated.

On Saturday mornings, I raced to clear breakfast dishes and do the laundry, I looked at Ryan. "Can I go now?"

He was building a DUPLO tower with Lexi in the family room. She was clapping. "Ok," he said. When one of us made the other one single-parent, we had to ask permission of the other.

I sprinted upstairs with the laptop, locking the door to our bedroom. Ryan would put Lexi down for her morning nap soon, then it would be time to get lunch ready when she woke up. I had only this time to myself, so I felt the pressure to be productive.

Perhaps Quan Âm's hand was on me, guiding me to find and re-fashion pieces of myself. My writing was something to work toward, a place to tuck myself away when the Dark Days creeped in. Perhaps this was her response to my prayers.

* * *

It was May and finally warm. The streets were washed of all the sand de-posited during winter storms. Buds grew on the trees. Green attempted to overtake brown. This was the time of spring before the prairie mosquitoes kept me indoors. I could play with Lexi in the backyard, smiling as she slid down the green plastic slide of the play structure, her head thrown back in fits of giggles.

I was still grateful to have a job.

I was still uncertain whether I might lose my job.

Months of fretful waking hours and night-time hours. I couldn't get my mind to stop running through the possibilities. Sleep was broken between Lexi's random wake-ups in the night and my alarm blaring at 6:10 a.m. for the workday. I frequently skipped lunch due to overlapping teleconferences, proceeded to devour an entire bag of Doritos at my desk before leaving work, then felt too sick to eat dinner.

While Ryan was out at soccer one evening, I put Lexi in her crib, her eyes fluttering closed, and finished washing dishes and cleaning the kitchen. Finally, I had time to myself before bedtime. I needed this time. Just as I was sitting down to hot tea and an inviting book, the landline rang. A slight twinge of panic made me frown. People texted. No one called the home line in the evenings.

"Can you meet me at the hospital?"

Ryan and a player on the opposing team had gone for the ball at the same time, crashing hard into each other.

Ryan underwent surgery the next morning, two pins put in his left ankle. After being at the hospital all day with Ryan, I came home to feed, bathe, and put Lexi to bed. Má had been with Lexi all day; she offered to stay but I could see her own exhaustion in her sagging shoulders. After Lexi was in bed, I fired up my work laptop, hot tea waiting beside me. I needed to finalize the interview questions and reference questions for a client manager for the next day.

Like a muscle overused, a part overworked, my mind was overtired. I attempted to bring my mind back to the moment of clarity I'd experienced when rocking Lexi to sleep while Inanna ascended back into the light, attempting to recreate it. Where was the hum deep inside?

Quan Âm, are you there?

Yet there was no moment to pause, to rest and to contemplate, to look through photo albums of my travels through sacred spaces, to reflect and refocus. I was drifting and grasping for a focal point.

Sitting reviewing interview questions, my brain was invaded with mind clutter. How would I manage my Athabasca course in creative non-fiction this upcoming weekend? How would I apply for the Manitoba Writers' Guild Mentorship Program for next year if I didn't have any new material? It ran January to June each year.

Ryan and I were also planning on trying for a baby next month. We were ready to grow our family. How would this work now? I was giving us a few months to conceive in order to have a baby born next spring or summer. Before the winter. Before Lexi's and Ryan's birthdays in late November. Before Christmas and New Year's. I did not want another winter baby.

I'd already planned to get the mentorship and deliver the baby sometime during that mentorship period. That would be challenging. But if I didn't apply for next year, if I waited another whole year, I would be on maternity leave for most of it and then returning to work. That would be more challenging. I also told myself I didn't want to lose the momentum from the Athabasca writing course I was going to start that upcoming weekend.

I had it all planned out. Ryan breaking his leg messed it all up.

* * *

"It's like someone died. It's silly." I wept to Ryan one night after putting Lexi to bed. Ryan sat and listened. "I don't even know why I'm crying, but it's like someone died. Who cries over a workplace?" He was stone, strong and steady, solid and unfailing, while I was water crashing over him, an uncontainable force.

Ryan was sitting on the couch beside me, his left leg lifted, his entire lower leg and ankle and foot encased in hardened black mesh. We were in the family room with Lexi's building blocks still jumbled in little piles on the rug, laundry still to be folded, dinner dishes still by the sink, and lunches still to be made for tomorrow.

"People who have been there for twenty or twenty-five years, chairing committees, spearheading initiatives, devoting their careers to making things better for the clients, now gone, their legacy forgotten, no longer relevant. Where did all that work go? How does it no longer matter? What is happening?" I wiped my tears with the hem of my T-shirt.

Ryan was not able to move, let alone go to the kitchen to get me some tissue. "I don't know. It's tough right now." He put his arm around me.

Quan Âm, where are you?

Despite my efforts, her light had yet to shine upon me. As the goddess of my ancestors, my chosen goddess, Quan Âm was still silent. The more I called out to her, the more elusive she became, and the further away I was from her, the more I sought her.

It was a strange space to inhabit: my role was to help employees go through transition, but I had my own transition to go through. These feelings and worries had been building for a while—what was a slow unravelling now left me coming undone quickly.

What about my own uncertainty and my sorrows? Where could that go, shoved aside while meeting with employees? I worried about whether I would lose my own job. I needed the mat leave benefits to have another baby. How could I not work there? But how could I keep working there?

The bits and pieces of myself I had sewn together with thread I found in sacred spaces began to loosen even further, fraying at the seams. What I had tried so hard to build, to seek, no longer made sense. But I kept wearing the pendant of Quan Âm, trying to focus on her light, focus on her shield against the Dark Days.

The corporate culture of care and service that had been modelled and encouraged by Old Management faded away when New Management was hired. The spirit of the Old Workplace embodied in the policies and organizational structure passed out of existence when policies were revised and the organization restructured to be the New Workplace.

I continued my rant to Ryan. "Those left on the management team are talking about having a wake for the office. So we can mourn together. Us left behind." I imagined all those left behind gathered in the large boardroom sharing stories of the golden days, clutching Kleenex, and boxing up physical objects that embodied the past—binders of telephone directories, thank-you card, and framed group photos taken at office team-building events.

"That's pretty bad." Ryan shifted his leg, continuously trying to find a more comfortable position.

Ryan was dealing with his own darkness, researching the internet about recovery time, and reading blog posts written by others who'd suffered the same injury. He was processing his own sorrow, grieving his independence. It was not just broken bones he was working through, but also a shattered sense of invincibility. He had not been out of the house in weeks except for check-ups at the doctor. I had to bathe him for the first week. When Má was at our house taking care of Lexi, she brought Ryan lunch as he sat on the couch distracting himself with Netflix. He was not able to walk or run or bike or drive, or go to work, all those activities that contributed to his self image.

We were both in mourning. Dark Days, now even darker after Ryan's injury, had invaded our home, tendrils of gloom crawling under doors, rounding corners, and creeping up the stairs to wrap around us as we slept. These tendrils clung to us, constricting and weighty. Not even Lexi, our light in human form, could shield us completely.

"The past is gone," I whispered to Ryan.

He rubbed my back, nodding.

"I don't know if I can let it go. I don't know if I can move on," I whispered, my voice cracking. I went to work every day and did my job like a good employee—adaptable, grateful to have a job. I needed to work for my daughter, like my mother needed to work for me. I needed to work if we wanted another baby.

The Workplace offered an employee assistance program which I didn't make use of. The Workplace sent out updates and communications which I didn't read. Was the Workplace trying to make improvements? I didn't pay attention if it was.

I began to remember the past at the Workplace as being better than it really was. I did not remember the bad or tough times. There were only good times of birthday cakes, excellent employee hires, and effective initiatives. I locked away the parts that were frustrating, had not worked. My Old Leader never made a mistake and he had all the answers. I had enjoyed every day at work, without question. My memories of the Old Workplace were re-writing themselves.

Just like when Má talked about Vietnam, she described the country she remembered from over thirty years ago, before we immigrated to Canada. Her homeland no longer existed as she remembered it. That country existed only in her memories. Just like Má, I was creating a shiny and untouchable past. The Old Workplace existed as Shambhala, a place of legend, idolized, perfect. The Shambhala of the Old Workplace existed only in my own mind.

The *me* that I had fashioned through visiting the underworld with Inanna was breaking apart. The remaining threads in my invisible garment were being tested and found lacking. What were Ba and Bà Ngoại saying from the afterlife? I couldn't hear them. I couldn't figure out how to channel King Arthur and Lê Lợi to become the hero in my own story.

I tucked myself under Ryan's arm and wrapped myself in him, a move made awkward by his leg elevated on a pillow. I wanted to absorb his energy and his strength. I had always depended on his steadiness, his clarity of purpose and being able to move ahead, face each day. But my life partner didn't have any energy to spare. I saw it in his eyes, staring past me, back to himself. He was turned inwards, focussed on his own loss. And I, as the one who had to bathe him and Lexi, who had to cook for him and Lexi, and had to take care of him and Lexi, had little of my own energy to give to him. These were even Darker Days as the two of us encased ourselves into our own respective bubbles, brushing up against but not able to penetrate each others' barriers.

"We all need a break," Ryan said, his voice confident. He was speaking to himself even more than he was to me. "The trip will be good for us."

We returned to Vietnam.

* * *

Lý Thái Tông, the Emperor of Vietnam in the 11th century, had no heir. Reaching back through his ancestors, the Emperor prayed to the Goddess of Mercy for a child, incense burning at her altar, his head touching the earth in a low bow before her.

Quan Âm, she who hears the cries of the world, turned one of her thousand eyes in his direction and stretched out one of her thousand arms to him. Slipping in between the mortal world and the glittering realm of nirvana, she entered the Emperor's dreams. Sitting on a single lotus flower emerging from water, the Goddess handed the Emperor a laughing baby boy. Shortly after that dream, the Emperor married a peasant woman and they had a son.

The Emperor had a pagoda built in honour of Quan Âm. It is supported by only one pillar, in homage to the single lotus from his dreams, as a symbol of his reverence and gratitude.

* * *

The pagoda is a square structure about fifteen feet across open on all sides, its wood painted glossy red and gold. It is set on a concrete pillar, rising out of the pond with stone stairs. Above its roof of layered curved ceramic tiles sit two bronze dragons guarding a large red disc between them. Inside the structure is a golden statue of a sitting Quan Âm, multiple arms outstretched behind her and two arms in front of her, palms together in the mudra for prayer. Eyes closed or eyes open, it was hard to tell, perhaps a trick of the light. Around the pagoda is a tranquil garden setting, the branches of trees sweeping gracefully down.

Chùa Một Cột—One Pillar Pagoda—is at the heart of Hà Nội. This was a replica of the pagoda Emperor Lý Thái Tông built almost a thousand years ago on this very site to honour Quan Âm.

We had been in Vietnam for a week now. This was time out of time, a chance to emerge from the shadows of the Dark Days in Winnipeg, a chance to let go of the breath we were holding in, a chance to escape back to the land of my ancestors for air and perspective. A pause in the chaos. A chance to recharge. I could already feel my shoulders loosening and my mind clearing.

I picked up a smooth grey rock from beside the steps and wrapped it in Kleenex to tuck away in my bag. I was still compelled to collect rocks on my travels.

The pagoda was a beauty in architecture born out of faith. A sacred space. Standing here, I felt so far removed from the daily grind of my new role at the Workplace, endless meetings, emails, and deadlines. And I could see this was a time of healing for Ryan. With physiotherapy and strong willpower, he was walking without a cane four months after his accident, although he limped when his muscles stiffened after sitting for an extended amount of time.

Ryan and I had escaped for a few days for our own romantic getaway in the north while Má and Jen looked after Lexi in the south. The centre of attention, Lexi was surrounded and spoiled by great-aunties and second cousins, all of them meeting her for the first time. She was beyond gleeful.

At age thirty-two, I was back in Vietnam. Five years earlier, I had brought my husband to walk the land where I was born for the first time. This time, I brought my child for the first time. With every return, there was a shift in my life, a new stage. And there was a shift in me—new eyes and new understanding. Since being in Vietnam five years previously, I had been on trips to other parts of the world, my travels through the sacred. After my transformative travels through Egypt and Greece and China and Scotland and England, I was experiencing Vietnam with different eyes. I was also travelling my new path as a mother. Vietnam had changed but so had I.

On this second trip to Hà Nội, I looked again for the Trưng sisters, their tale opening up my connection to my ancestors. Their blood still nourishing the earth after two thousand years. Ryan and I relaxed on the second-floor balcony of a café overlooking the Lake of the Restored Sword. The honking from the ocean of Hondas on the streets below serenaded us. I took a sip of my trà đá. I asked Ryan if he could spot the Golden Tortoise that had asked Emperor Lê for the return of the Will of Heaven sword. The lake shimmered black glass reflecting the neon lights in a light breeze. Ryan stared at me and I stared at him, our pupils dilating, the air changing between us, heating up. I recognized he was not just my co-parent and my housemate, but my chosen life partner. I remembered the layers of our many shared experiences and of our connection. I remembered love.

One Pillar Pagoda had made an impression on me seven years ago when I had toured the country for the first time after the end of the mourning period for Bà Ngoại. I was excited to bring Ryan here now and excited to return myself. Seven years ago, I did not ask anything of Quan Âm. I was just discovering the divine feminine then.

Like last time, a steady queue of worshippers walked up and down the steps, joss sticks in their hands and prayers on their lips. Worshippers took turns praying in front of the altar and leaving their joss sticks in the urn, the incense carrying their hopes and pleas up to heaven.

I took Ryan's hand up the steep steps. The spicy smell of incense grew stronger as we approached the altar.

The sun was high in the sky; it was the hottest time of the day. I felt my feet beneath me. My dress clung to my skin, droplets of sweat damp on my back and pooling between my breasts. Quan Âm hung heavily around my neck. The humidity wrapped itself around me like a warm quilt. The air was fragrant with mature blossoms mixed with wet earth and ladies' perfumes. Birdsong became gentle background music. I had no joss sticks, just the intentions in my heart. I did not feel like a fake this time.

I focussed on my breath. I pushed all thoughts outward from my mind and thought only of my goddess radiant and calm. "She who hears the cries of the world." I grasped the pendant of Quan Âm between my fingers, touching the indentations and the cold grooves. I tried to stare past the golden statue of my goddess. An inner glow from the gold, like a radiant inner light, reached me. I tried to steady my breath and transfix it in my spirit. Envisioning tiny hands grasping my fingers and sparkling eyes searching my face, I concentrated. Lexi playing big sister to a sibling. My life unfolding the way I planned.

"Quan Âm, please give me a baby to add to our family." I bowed my head in reverence.

I did not feel her presence but perhaps the wind carried my message to Quan Âm wherever she was that day. Perhaps, whether I knew it or not, one of her thousand eyes was focussed on me at that moment and one of her thousand arms did hold out a hand at my back.

The day after we came back home to Winnipeg, the pregnancy test was positive. Even though she had been silent, she had indeed heard my prayers. Quan Âm had blessed me.

The pregnancy bubbled up in my mind as a delicious secret, a jewel of information tight in my grasp. We would wait until the first trimester was over before announcing it to the world. But we told Má and Jen and Ryan's parents. We told close friends. Time was measured once again in weeks, week four, week five, week six an embryo—little Embry. The size of a sesame seed. Then a pea. Then a peanut. I was happily repeating all the milestones as I had when pregnant with Lexi.

I could now hold on at work for another few months more easily. My pregnancy was a balm. I chose to think positively and plan that I would get accepted into the writing mentorship for next year. I would be on maternity leave and I would write. After I returned to work, who knew what the Workplace would be like. Who knew what I would be like then. My garment, while weather-beaten by the Dark Days of work and personal pressures, still held together, and the threads while frayed, held strong.

I had it all planned out.

Endings

When Moses led the Israelites out of Egypt, he parted the Red Sea to allow the Israelites safe passage. There was no going back. The only way to move would be forward.

The Old Workplace had passed away. An ache in my heart, an emptiness, lodged inside me. I had given my heart to my work family. And still, a deep fear and uncertainty – will I lose my job? The Old Workplace existed only in my own mind.

Growing Embry week after week, my mind merrily meandered to the possibilities of the future. I just needed to hold on, to do my job, my new job, for the next few months, and be thankful to have a job.

I called on Quan Âm as my chosen goddess, with her mercy and compassion, and gentle power, to calm my spirit through the Dark Days. She was the conscious choice for a spiritual focal point, grounding me back to my roots for inspiration.

I had to let go of the past.

Five: The Wilderness

"WHAT ARE YOU WORKING ON TODAY, L234?" a colleague came by my workstation to ask me.

"Nothing that will matter, D600." I laughed, wrapping my cardigan more tightly around me to conceal my swelling belly.

"That's for sure. It doesn't matter."

This terrible inside joke my colleague and I shared comforted me and made me angry at the same time. I felt as though I was watching someone else act out these scenes, and I knew it was not productive, but I wasn't able to stop doing it. It wasn't me. I was usually the one who brought up the positives in any situation, the silver linings. I had learned in my work in HR to reframe the situation and change my perspective. Not now. I had become a stranger to myself, unable to stop.

D600 had been at the Workplace longer than I had. She remembered the Old Workplace. As did I. Today we shared laughs. Last week, we shared tears.

"I don't know what's going on," she said, sitting at my workstation last week.

"I don't think anyone does. Everyone is lost."

No one seemed to know what was going to happen next. We all acted in ways that were surprising to us.

My identity was wrapped up in familiar garments of the past. Expressing frustration and nostalgia allowed me to hold those garments close again, shielding me from the blowing winds of transformation. I could not shed these garments, nor did I really want to. My negative speech and negative actions kept the past alive. If I tried to move on, I was pulled back by my colleagues reminding me of what used to be. If my co-workers began to move on, I reminded them of what used to be, pulling them back. It was comforting to relive the wonderful past and commiserate about how terrible it was in the present. I told myself I just needed to survive the next six months, then the baby would arrive, and I would be on maternity leave.

The situation was made infinitely harder by the fact that, while I occupied the same physical space, it wasn't the same place. My New Leader sat in my Old Leader's office. Ghosts wandered the halls, wandering around empty workstations. Our departed colleagues became the lost souls, the lost spirits haunting us who were still here.

During the Festival of the Hungry Ghosts in Buddhist tradition, ghosts wander the earth, haunting the living. The living offer food, and burn money and incense, to appease the ghosts. I was feeding those ghosts with negative speak and negative actions. I couldn't stop.

I began to walk a different route to the lunchroom to avoid the old Central Depository unit. There were so many empty workstations of former colleagues who haunted the spaces with their absence, with their silence. That workstation in that corner, which had always been decked out with finger-paintings done by my colleague's grandchildren, now looked sterile. I used to take a caramel from the candy dish of my colleague who occupied the workstation in the front row.

The workplace became a void—an otherworld, a shadow world where no light or darkness existed, merely a suspension of energy. This was the space in-between, after an exhale and before an inhale. I feared being swallowed up by the ghosts if I continued to wander for too much longer.

* * *

One day at work, I went to the washroom and there in the toilet—tiny pink spots, droplets that began to swirl and disperse in the water. I flushed quickly, getting rid of the evidence. That wasn't. It couldn't be. As with my pregnancy with Lexi, under my dark loose clothing, my breasts swelled and my abdomen hardened beneath skin and fatty tissue. I often touched my bump throughout the day, still my delicious secret. I had exercised that day, lots of squats and lunges. Perhaps I'd loosened or torn something?

I pulled on my boots and my jacket. I would need my parka soon, the deep chill of the coming winter evident in the brittleness of the air. Despite not wanting to turn my attention to it, a nugget of doubt, of fear, burrowed inside me. Could the pink spots have been imaginary, something wrong with my eyes or with my contacts? I should throw away these old lenses.

I was almost twelve weeks pregnant, tired and nauseous and joyful.

"Don't jump to conclusions. Stay home tomorrow and take it easy," Ryan said that night. Was that worry I saw in his eyes?

There was more spotting every time I used the washroom.

When I told Má, she told me not to worry. Was her voice too controlled and cheery? She was the worrier in the family, reminding me to drink water, to sleep, to take my vitamins, so when she told me not to worry, something was definitely wrong.

I called the obstetrician the next morning. I hadn't attended my first appointment yet, as doctors only schedule an appointment after the first trimester.

"I exercised. Does that matter?" I asked.

"I'm not worried. Tomorrow, come in and you can hear the heartbeat, or I'll send you for an ultrasound."

"Is there anything I can do?" I was desperate for a quick solution.

"Either the bleeding will stop, or it will become more. Wait."

So I sat in the family room, peppermint tea cupped between both hands, snuggled in a blanket, the mid-day light shimmering in through the window. Orange rays fell lightly on plush pillows giving a wondrous luminous quality to those ordinary objects. I could rarely enjoy this time of day at home: either I was at work or chasing after Lexi. And I was even more rarely alone at home, wrapped in silence.

It was only last week, on a quick family trip to Minneapolis, Má had been splashing with Lexi in the hotel pool, while I floated around, weightless. Ears submerged underwater, listening to the silence. I wished I was back there now.

On Flickr I swiped through some family photos, from last week, from Halloween when Lexi dressed up in her alligator-dinosaur-dragon costume, and from Vietnam. I stared at pictures of Chùa Một Cột and remembered my prayers to Quan Âm a couple of months ago, I had walked the same land as the Trưng sisters, from my ancestors, to Bà Ngoại, to me, to Embry inside me. The stillness. The calm. I wished I was back there now.

I could almost believe this was just a relaxing day at home, a day to myself, enjoying the light outside and the warmth within, to recharge from the stress of the Workplace. Weather forecasters were predicting that the upcoming winter would be just as cold as last winter, so this day could be an indulgence to gather strength for the coming chill, for when life stood still, frosted over again. I could almost believe that. Except I had to put on a maxi pad around lunchtime as red streaks and clots replaced the pink spots.

I rubbed the rock I had picked up at Chùa Một Cột, reminding myself of the day we prayed to Quan Âm there.

Please. Please. Don't let it be that.

***

Long ago, Quan Âm lived as princess Miao Shan in China. The king ordered her to marry but she refused and found sanctuary as a nun in a Buddhist temple. He ordered the nuns to give Miao Shan the most menial tasks. When he found out she completed her tasks with a light heart, he was furious. He ordered her execution. At the moment she was to be beheaded, a white tiger appeared and carried her off.

***

Twenty-four hours after seeing the pink spots, my lower abdomen began to cramp. Maybe I had indigestion. I hadn't eaten as I normally did, and I wasn't walking around as I normally did. After a couple hours, it stopped. There, I was fine, I tried to convince myself. Bright red blood.

I couldn't make it to the washroom fast enough. I stood up from the toilet leaving the whole bowl a bright crimson mess. Fresh like from an open wound.

Má stayed with Lexi while I got into the car with Ryan, his dinner half eaten. I couldn't even look at my daughter as I was leaving. I didn't know what she could tell from my face and I didn't want to scare her. I couldn't look at Má, a sympathetic look from her and I would start crying.

On the way to the ER, I said to Ryan, "My cramping's stopped. I feel fine now. Like it's done. Like what was supposed to happen is now done."

"We're pretty sure what it is," he responded.

Neither one of us spoke the word *miscarriage*. As if saying the word out loud would give it power to manifest into reality.

The triage nurse at St. Boniface Hospital took down my information and gave me a pamphlet. I had delivered Lexi at St. B.

"If you're having a miscarriage, and I'm not saying you are. If you are, there's nothing we can do. The waiting room is pretty full tonight."

"What would you do if you were us?" Ryan asked the nurse.

"I can't say. You can go or stay."

"What would you do?" he asked again.

She paused. "I'd go to a different ER with a shorter waiting time."

Walking from the parking lot up the stairs at Grace Hospital, I had another gush and felt hot liquid fill my underwear, soak through my black sweatpants, and drip down my left leg.

I went to the single stall washroom to clean myself up. I threw my blood-soaked pad into the metal trash bin screwed to the green tile wall. Its own weight caused it to sink to the bottom of the bin. Blood started to drip from the seams of the metal bin and formed a pool on the green linoleum floor below. It was like a scene from a horror movie.

"You can sit down," the intake nurse told me when it was our turn at the desk.

"I can't."

"No, you have to sit down." Her tone was sharper this time.

"I can't. I don't want to make the chair dirty."

The intake nurse put down a white sheet for me to sit on. "Now sit."

Sure, that wasn't noticeable at all. I was annoyed by this breach of my privacy. Any onlooker in the ER could guess: a woman of my age with blood stains and a concerned partner hovering close by.

"Take them to the gynie room," the intake nurse finally told the ER nurse.

"I'm going to be outside when they examine you," Ryan stated.

"No, stay."

While we waited for the exam and for my blood test results to come back, I Googled "bleeding at twelve weeks pregnancy." I read blog post after blog post about women having excessive bleeding, yet at the hospital, they still heard the heartbeats of their tiny miracles.

**

Miao Shan made her home on Fragrant Mountain. She meditated there for many years.

One day, the king fell ill and doctors could not cure him. A monk said he could make life-saving medicine from the arms and the eyes of a person if freely given. The king doubted any such person existed.

The monk went to Fragrant Mountain to ask Miao Shan and she willingly agreed.

After he recovered, the king made a pilgrimage to the mountain to offer his thanks. Looking at the now-mutilated figure, he knew it was his daughter Miao Shan.

**

A doctor, a medical student, and a nurse came in to start the internal exam. I looked up at the ceiling, wishing I could float away, be anywhere but here.

Ryan was sitting close to my head and touched my shoulder. I couldn't touch him back. I knew if I did or if I even looked at him, I would break. I needed to focus on the medical procedure taking place. If I let my mind think of anything else, I would shatter.

The doctor was done. "It's very unlikely your pregnancy will progress, with your cervix open and that amount of blood. Also, your HCG levels are much lower than a woman who is twelve weeks along. This is all consistent with a first trimester miscarriage. It was nothing you did. Miscarriages are fairly common, and women go on to have healthy pregnancies afterwards. Maybe you will pass the tissue tonight. We will keep you for observation overnight."

The sentences all flowed together, without a pause, without true concern. It was a script he had said to so many women before me.

The doctor, the medical student, and the nurse left.

My mind felt blank and cluttered at the same time, stuffed with cotton that was both dense and weightless as air.

Ryan and I held each other, my body shaking.

"I'm sorry." I was barely able to get the words out. It felt like something I should say.

My salty tears stained his grey hoodie. We whispered words to each other to bring each other comfort. Throughout our years together, we had been bound by so much joy, now we were forever bound by this too. Shared loss. Shared sorrow.

The nurse came back to clean me up. "I'm sorry for your news."

I blinked away the tears. "Thank you." How many times would I have to tell people the news and say thank you?

A couple of hours later, I told Ryan to go home. There was nothing else to be done. Má and Jen were with Lexi and he had to get home to her.

The garment of mine, of myself, began to rip along the seams, but also in random patches. The threads I had collected and used to stitch myself together were not proving strong enough.

* * *

The king fell to his knees and asked for forgiveness.

Giving up human eyes and giving up human arms, Miao Shan told her father she no longer felt pain.

When she began her journey to nirvana, she heard the cries from people on earth and felt their suffering. Filled with compassion, she returned to earth as the Goddess of Mercy, vowing never to leave until such time as all suffering had ended.

＊＊＊

I was alone that night in the ER. I usually had my husband and daughter under the same roof with me.

The ER was noisy with footsteps, medical beeps, and voices of staff.

Where I was, it was silent.

The ER was bright with halogen lights and electronic screens.

Where I was, it was dark.

I felt a tightening of my chest, a shortness of breath. Hot tears rolled down my face. All the emotions I had shut away for the last couple days bubbled over the edge. When we had entered the hospital, I had taken a step back as if watching a movie, but now I stepped into myself again. This was really happening to me.

I was alone.

I thought of Quan Âm and remembered praying to her at Chùa Một Cột. I was pregnant but I didn't know it then. She hadn't been there that day at the pagoda.

From my hospital bed, I called out to Quan Âm. *My goddess, save me from this pain. Take it all away.* She HAD to come to me now.

I imagined her in her flowing robes turning away from the glittering light of nirvana, hearing my cries, and moving towards me. Gazing at me with serene eyes and a comforting smile, she would say, "My child, I am here, fear not." She would reveal great truths to me and bring me peace. I imagined her soft palm upon my cheek and that touch would warm my spirit and chase away my sorrow. She would lighten my burden of pain. What I could not bear alone, she would take away.

I waited.

The ER stayed noisy with footsteps, medical beeps, and voices of staff. The ER stayed bright with halogen lights and electronic screens.

For me there was only silence and darkness.

Quan Âm did not reveal herself and her light did not shine on me.

I needed her and she didn't come.

＊＊＊

Subject: My Absence
Hi All,

I debated whether or not I wanted to write this email, but I decided I wanted to tell you. I was going to share my happy news with you very soon, instead I have bad news to share. I had a miscarriage on Wednesday. I would have been 12 weeks pregnant. I spent Wednesday night in the ER and the doctors confirmed it yesterday and I came home.

I'm ok physically. We are devastated. It just wasn't meant to be. I'm thankful for all the support around me. I just didn't want to pretend that I'm ok when I'm not when I come back to work, and I didn't want to pretend that nothing changed in my life.

Hoping to see you all Monday but I'll have to see.

I know you'll all be supportive, and I thank you in advance,
Linda

—

Subject: Sad News
Hey best friend,

We are devastated. I know it wasn't meant to be, but it will take time for the pain to become manageable. One of the difficult parts is to now tell everyone our sad news.

I am looking forward to Lexi's birthday on Wednesday and her party on Sunday, something to focus on. Please do not mention anything on Sunday as a lot of my extended family didn't know.

I know you'll be supportive and I thank you in advance,
Linda

* * *

Sitting on our bed, I yanked another Kleenex from the box. My nose always ran when I cried. "You weren't here," I shouted at Ryan.

He leaned against the wall facing me. He shook his head. "I'm always around. This was not usual."

Lexi was playing on her iPad on the floor between us, playing songs.

"I went to bed alone all those nights." My voice shook. Wasn't anger a stage of grief?

"We already had plans." Ryan had gotten together with a friend who was in from out of town the night after I came home from the hospital. Then the next night he went to a housewarming party. Ryan had told everyone I couldn't go to the party because I had a cold.

"And why would you cancel, right?" I asked. "You weren't here." I wanted to see him hurt like I hurt.

The burning palms of loss and the hot breath of grief accompanied me to a place I had never been before. Má said the little one didn't want to stay with us, so there was nothing I could do. It wasn't meant to be.

I knew it was not productive, but I could not stop it. It wasn't me. I became a stranger to myself, unable to stop. Since Quan Âm had not shown me any compassion, it seemed like I had no compassion for anyone. I was further away from her and her qualities I wanted to embody than ever before.

There was a dimness in the hazel flecks of his irises, and a tightness around his mouth. He crossed his arms in front of him, a barrier between us. He shook his head again. "We were out together during the day. Everyone grieves differently."

Lexi looked up from her iPad, her wide eyes and long eyelashes beautiful. She wore white pyjamas, the ones we had bought in Vietnam for a few dollars. White. While white is the colour of innocence in North American culture, it is the colour of mourning in Vietnamese culture. I remembered wearing the white headband across my temples for Ba and for Bà Ngoại. Mourning.

I wanted Ryan to shield me, to hold me, and whisper soothing words to me. I didn't want to be strong and independent. I wanted to crumple and be cocooned in care.

Ryan came to sit on the bed. He left a space between us. Lexi held her arms up for me to hold her. I lifted her up and she fit in that space.

The Neutral Zone

Moses and the Israelites wandered the wilderness for forty years. The people had no sense of belonging, worshipped golden idols, and behaved strangely. This was the space in-between what once was and what was yet to be, between the past and the new potential.

I did not know my place or my role at the Workplace. I became a stranger to myself. I did things and said things that were not me, yet I could not stop. I spoke poorly of the Workplace and spread despair and cynicism, contributing to a toxic work environment.

A haunted face stared back at me in the mirror after the miscarriage. I became a stranger to myself. I did things and said things that were not me, yet I could not stop. I yelled at Lexi, picked fights with Ryan, berated Má, and took advantage of Jen. I turned away from them.

Quan Âm did not reveal herself to me. She was not there to walk with me through the place of shadows. My prayers went unanswered when I called for divine intervention. The light of the sacred did not flicker inside me. My Goddess of Mercy had no compassion for me.

How long would I be lost?

Subject: RE: My Absence

Oh Linda (((Hugs))) I am sooo sad to hear that news – you are such a great Mom! We care so much about you, tears rolling down my face as I type …

Take care, and be sure and take as much time as you need, we are always here for you. 😊 *– The HR family <3 <3 <3*

A week after spending the night in the ER, I sat at my workstation, staring at my computer, scrolling through hundreds of emails, taunted by the flashing red light on my phone indicating unheard voicemails. I prepared to write a new to-do list.

My water bottle was how I had left it mid-week last week, beside my phone, the spout still up, the container half full. I drank from it and the water tasted stagnant, like what I imagined the taste of standing water to be that bred hardy Manitoba mosquitoes. I threw out the plastic bag containing my week-old slice of cinnamon raisin bread, dry and sprouting the first buds of mould spores. My gym bag, now funky smelling, was where I had left it on the floor next to my filing cabinet in my haste to rush home last week. *I exercised, does that matter?* I remembered saying to my OB last week.

Everything was more-or-less how I'd left it. As though no time had passed at all. As though I hadn't lived a lifetime that past week.

I started my emails to client managers and employees: *I apologize for the delay in response. I was away unexpectedly from the office ...*

I did not speak to anyone on the phone, not trusting my voice. I avoided my calls and I answered all voicemails with an email: *Further to the voicemail you left for me last week, I was away unexpectedly ...*

Those lines both disclosed so little and yet contained so much.

I wore the same black pants, stretchy black tank top and cranberry knit cardigan that I had worn last week. I even wore the same black maternity bra I wore last week. Last week, the dark clothing and cardigan were to conceal my swelling belly, so that my body would not give away my secret until I was ready to make my joyful announcement. This week, my body had not changed much since it had started to thicken with Embry, with breasts still tender and belly still enlarged. The bump was different, squishy instead of firm now that there was no occupant. This week, my body was a reminder of what I wanted to forget.

Colleagues hugged me when I walked in, followed by a round of *I'm sorrys* and *thank yous*. Is that why women didn't share their happy news so early, because then they might have to give an update with sad news? To have to go back to all the people who hugged me and congratulated me and then see pity in their eyes and say thank you, that was the risk.

I was not myself. The garment of myself was torn and ripped, not a gentle fraying at the edges from too much wear and tear and usage, but decisive slicing through the fabric, sharp cuts that were not likely to be mendable.

* * *

At Lexi's second birthday party, I felt so tense that someone who KNEW would give me a sympathetic look, and I would crumple, bits and pieces in tatters leaving loose threads floating through the air.

After the initial outpouring of support, life went back to normal for the people I'd told. Did they assume my life was back to equilibrium then?

I noticed people were uncomfortable with sad news—"I'm so sorry for your loss"—and then silence. They did not know what to say. I did not want to make others uncomfortable. And I did not want to be disappointed in the reactions of others, to expect something more, so that I was saddened further.

Ask me how I am.

Hug me.

Ask me to talk about it again, to share my story again.

Instead, a shift in body posture, a wriggling of the hands, eyes downcast, was the usual response. And who really wanted to hear about it all, the graphic bloody details and the deep pain.

It felt like pretending nothing had happened was the thing I should be doing.

I snuggled with my friend's three-month-old baby girl at the party, her sweet lips curling into a smile as she slept. My friend knew about our loss, but never let on, as I had asked her to do when I emailed her. She smiled and I smiled. Who knew we were both such fine actresses? We had all been at dim sum a few weeks ago when we had shared our happy news that I was ten weeks pregnant. Hugs all around while Lexi and their older son watched iPad together. My friend was cradling her new daughter, I was expecting, there was so much excitement around the table. We treated ourselves to white translucent dumplings, deep-fried crispy dumplings, and silky mango pudding. This sweet memory now tasted bitter.

At her birthday party, Lexi stroked the baby's cheeks.

"Gentle, gentle," I whispered to my daughter.

I felt a dull ache inside me. I wanted her to be a big sister.

In my line of sight were Má and my mother-in-law, watching. Were those looks of concern? Wistful looks for what might have been? Jen was nearby, taking care of the logistics so I could enjoy the party.

It would have been the perfect time to announce my pregnancy.

Hello, everyone. Can I say something before we eat? Thank you all for coming to celebrate Lexi's birthday. It means so much to us to have our family and friends around us. Ryan and I have another reason to celebrate with everyone ... Lexi is going to be a big sister! We're expecting!!!

Everyone would have clapped and cheered. I would have given the baby back to my friend before she got crushed between the hugs and kisses and congratulations.

Instead I handed the baby back to my friend and excused myself to escape to the washroom before the tears could form. I blew my nose, flushed the toilet, and smiled in the mirror, clenching and unclenching my fists before I opened the door.

Should I have cancelled the party? Lexi was two, what did she care about a party? Ryan read her a book in the corner of the family room for most of the party anyway—shielding her from overstimulation. Then who was the party for?

Má had told me "don't tell anyone." Did she believe our family would think I brought this on myself? That my miscarriage reflected poorly on me and therefore on her and Jen too? A weakness or a defect of some kind. Poor health or poor genes. If I had cancelled the party, people would have had questions. People would talk. Would they judge? Would they even care? I had to go on with the party so that no one knew anything was different. In my family, we always wanted to show the best of ourselves. We saved face, as I think is common for Vietnamese families. What would happen if instead of saving face, we could show we were flawed, scared, hurt sometimes? We could all lean on each other. We could connect.

"Thanks for coming to the party." I hugged my cousin's wife.

"Thanks for inviting us," she said into my hair.

"How are you?"

"Good. And you?" she asked me.

Well, I had a miscarriage just a few days ago and I'm barely holding it together. The aftershock of work challenges threatens my mental health. "Good. Busy with work and Lexi, of course. What's new with you?" I smiled, nodding my head over and over.

Why did I do this to myself? Put on this show?

Was I trying to focus on the positive, and move on with my life? Was it a way to pull myself out of the darkness, to force myself to get better? It could be seen as a healthy approach to provide closure, something to focus on. A happy exterior.

Or was this a rush to heal, pushing aside the feelings, not giving them their proper due, not honouring what once was, what was important and meant so much? I was screaming on the inside. Screaming to be real, to be authentic. It took so much emotional labour to hide all that. To be shiny and presentable.

We had fifty people in our house at the party—extended family and close friends—the space brimming over with life. I was surrounded by the people I loved most in the world, and my secret miscarriage was a barrier, separating me from everyone.

Why do we women wait to announce their pregnancy? I wondered. The risk of miscarriage decreases significantly after the first trimester, so we wait. But it takes emotional labour to hold in the deepest all-thought consuming joy, to grasp that tightly inside. Is it worth it? There is emotional work required to conceal bodily changes, trips to the bathroom, excuses for missed days at work, made-up stories for changes to diet and drinking habits. For what? Just so that you do not have to share your deepest pain if you do experience pregnancy loss. There is emotional labour required to have to conceal your pain, paint over it with forced smiles and spin tales of stomach bugs and exhaustion. You are trapped in an endless cycle of concealment, of being inauthentic. I screamed. I did not want to pretend, I wanted to be myself.

Miscarriage is so common—one in five pregnancies. And we hide it. To make something so normal so secretive, eliminates the space for any woman to talk about it. Not only did I have to deal with the loss itself, as another layer, I also had to deal with concealing the loss. It is all wrong. Any kind of concealment of your true self, of your true reality, takes more energy and more willpower. And it takes something from you, to not be able to talk about it in real terms. You pay for it. While I would not have announced to a bus driver or to a grocery store clerk that I'd just had a miscarriage, I would have liked to have shared with the people who I knew cared about me.

And how often do people paint on a smile, answer "fine" to questions, all the while feeling the cracks underneath the surface? We only brush up against each other's lives. We do not connect.

I didn't let anyone talk to me about it. The end of the party became an invisible threshold, a closure to my grief. Like I was over it. Like I should get over it. I only realized afterward that I needed to talk about it. But it was too late. I had made the miscarriage an unspeakable thing. I did it to myself. I had isolated myself.

Change is external. Change is situational. Change may be fast.

Transition is internal. Transition is psychological. Transition may be slow.

The cost of keeping the secret was high. The pieces of myself I gave away, I could never recover. And the worst part, I did it to myself, I undid myself. Miscarriage happened to me but I was the one who silenced myself.

Out of everything, that was my regret.

* * *

Grief was not linear. Days passed, and I was fine. Then I saw a woman swollen with pregnancy in an elevator—and couldn't help but think I would have been that big now. Why me? I cried again and was surprised by my tears. I regretted the renewed grief that sent me back into that dark place. Why didn't Quan Âm come when I cried out to her? Then I regretted my arrogance at thinking it was all about me. Lexi played with her baby doll and I touched my belly, my throat tightening. She told me she loved me and I felt thankful for all that I had. Acquaintances asked me when I would be having another one, said I wouldn't want them too far apart, and I screamed on the inside, but smiled on the outside.

I had honoured my pregnancy privately. When we'd visited Minneapolis just a few days before the miscarriage, I had bought myself a bracelet. It was a solid half circle of plated rose gold with a heart full of glittering glass, and a soft maroon cord on the other side to complete the circle. It symbolized the spark. An umbilical cord, life cord—potential. Rose gold—precious. Intended as my talisman and my symbol of my love for the spark, I wore the bracelet at Lexi's party in silent and personal remembrance. The spark hadn't been enough to ignite, to grow stronger, for the light to become brighter. But it was enough to be real, to be acknowledged, to be remembered and mourned, now tucked away only in a corner of my heart. It would never be forgotten but the ache was not as raw.

One month after the miscarriage, the red blood came again. I had never entirely stopped bleeding during that time but now it came in gushes and globs. I sent Ryan to Shopper's for extreme maxi pads so I would not leak through my sweatpants again at the hospital.

Here we were, back at the ER at Grace Hospital. Here I was … again. The continuation of a nightmare. My body was doing strange things still.

We were told to take a seat. While in the waiting room, as I began to pass out, the world faded to black. Ryan and a nurse were right there, wheeled out a bed, I was told to get on but couldn't.

Darkness.

The feeling of being lifted.

Muffled voices and cold hands.

The space in-between losing consciousness and regaining consciousness.

Floating. Aimless. Wandering.

I was suspended in an abyss, but not necessarily an emptiness. The space was filled with something, and I was being suffocated by it, thick, but unknown. I could have lived a lifetime in that moment.

Bloodletting. Lifeforce. Landing.

The darkness lifted. A small pinhole in the centre of the black movie screen widened until it filled my entire view.

"You're back. Do you know your name?" someone asked as she took my blood pressure.

"Hmmm." I paused. The knowledge was hard to grasp. "Linda."

"Do you know where you are, Linda?"

"Hmmm." The knowledge was closer. "At the hospital ER?"

"Your husband said you have a doctor's appointment tomorrow."

"Yes, with an OB-GYN. I had a miscarriage a month ago and my bleeding never completely stopped."

"The IV gave you back some fluids. Looks like they're helping. Nothing else we can do for you. Best to go home and see the doctor tomorrow."

The next morning, I was waiting for Dr. Y at his downtown clinic. My original plan had been to pop over to his office from work, take an hour or so for the doctor to say everything was fine, just takes time to heal, and then send me away, back to work for a productive afternoon. Passing out from blood loss at the ER the night before had not been in my plans.

Dr. Y was efficient and moved around his office quickly and methodically. I told my story again. His matter-of-fact attitude actually made it easier for me to talk about these things that were so personal and painful.

I'd been a volunteer birth control and pregnancy counsellor at a feminist pro-choice women's clinic when Ryan and I were first married, and part of the role was to describe the procedure of a therapeutic abortion so that a woman was fully informed. The dilation and curettage procedure could be manual or could require a machine to remove the products of conception.

Dr. Y never said what he was doing down there, but it did feel like the sweeping motions I had used in theory to describe the procedure.

"You're doing a good job. Pain ok?" he asked me, my feet still in stirrups.

"I'm ok," I said to the ceiling.

"That should do it." He had a small glass bottle. "It looks like a grasshopper." The doctor commented. "Should be fine now."

Dr. Y never said what was inside the bottle. The grasshopper was obviously remaining tissue, remaining products of conception.

It was good to know my bleeding was caused by something. And now could my uterus heal?

"How long do you recommend until we can start trying for a baby again?"

"Wait at least one full menstrual cycle."

The clock was ticking, and this was just another setback. Winter solstice was a few days away, the earth spinning toward the longest darkness of the year. I had already been counting time in months, in menstrual cycles, in moon cycles since Ryan broke his leg. If we waited until after January, and conceived in February or March, I would have a baby in October or November. I had already told myself I did not want a winter baby again. These thoughts rolled around in my mind constantly, the distracting stories I told myself.

* * *

I had thought my pregnancy served as the boundary event, the point of no return to Egypt. I should have known better. That was too easy. I should have known that would not be enough. The boundary event needed to be decisive. Something of value needed to be sacrificed. Throughout history, a bloodletting in human and animal form had been common, before battle, before the harvest, to appease goddesses and gods, to show one's devotion. There had been great loss of life when Moses parted the Red Sea. Miao Shan gave up much.

I now realized the miscarriage, not the pregnancy, was the boundary event. It was my blood sacrifice. To move forward, I'd had to give up something meaningful. What I did not realize was that the price would be so high.

The Israelites spent forty years in the wilderness. How long before I could be pregnant again? How long could I continue with my job as it was? How long until Quan Âm shone her light upon me? The ghosts of the wilderness were threatening to gobble me up and carry me off to the shadowlands. The garment of my snipped and torn self, after walking with Inanna, was now burned away, neither recognizable nor salvageable.

My idea of the wilderness I had to cross was not the land Charlton Heston walked through in Technicolor, red desert on the sound stage, dusty and barren. I envisioned instead an expanse of silver light softly glowing. No land to touch one's feet to, no sky to look up to, no points of reference at all. As I moved within the space, I did not know where I'd just come from or where I needed to go next. No beginning or end to feel, no top or bottom, no edges to push against. As I moved, I breathed the silver into my lungs and it filled my body until I twinkled and shimmered like the space around me. I didn't transform into silver light to dissolve into my surroundings, I kept my own form. I began to crystalize, forming solid crystals glittering like diamonds in my hair, in my eyes, along my skin. I wondered if my crystalized self would prove to be stronger, more resilient to thrive under pressure, channel energies and bring about healing. To cross the wilderness was to be subjected to this transformation.

Six: The Promised Land (?)

New Beginnings

Moses did not enter the Promised Land. He had fulfilled his destiny. A new identity, with a new sense and a new energy, was needed.

Sitting at my workstation, it was the same physical space, and yet it wasn't the same place. I had mourned the Old Workplace. The New Workplace was emerging. Who would I be at the New Workplace? Would I be able to adapt to the expectations of the New Workplace? I had to have faith. My new self was a spark that waited to grow bright.

Miscarrying revealed to me the preciousness of life. Having a child would be that much sweeter knowing and appreciating the struggles. I had faith I would have the child I was meant to have. I practised patience, everyday. Some days I failed. I practised. The pregnancy I lost had been a spark. That spark didn't have enough power to grow, for the light to become brighter.

Faith meant always believing. I had faith that I would have the connection I was meant to have with Quan Âm. The moment Quan Âm shone her sacred light on me would be that much brighter because it was so hard won. I practised patience, everyday. Some days I failed. I practised. Quan Âm's sacred light existed as a spark. This spark waited to be lit, to grow, to glow brightly.

I worked for the spark that would catch fire.

My weight never went down after the miscarriage in November. At Christmas, I was five pounds heavier than usual. The weight clung to my body and no matter what I did, it would not shake off. A layer of fat like insulation created a barrier and became both comforting and isolating. My body still betrayed me, leftover hormones still firing off. I continued to take a prenatal vitamin every day, go to yoga and to the gym for cardio, and eat lean protein. I continued to plan for a baby.

I was pushing the re-set button. Second child—Take Two. Dr. Y said to wait one complete normal menstrual cycle before trying again. To have to wait a couple of months until February to try and conceive again was like telling me Christmas morning had been cancelled and moved to another date, and by the way, it may be delayed a month after that, and maybe another month after that. There was unrest in my heart, a desire to get on with it. Life was now measured in moon cycles—it was waning gibbous moon and I had to wait from last quarter, to waning crescent, to dark moon, to waxing crescent, to first quarter, to waxing gibbous, to full moon, to waning gibbous again and then one more complete cycle after that. I needed a new pregnancy to fill the chasm that the miscarriage bomb had created in me. Could I make this feeling go away? This holding pattern. This uncertainty. I needed to grasp control of my life again. The fact that I wasn't pregnant but wanted to be pregnant consumed my thoughts. It was not in me to be patient with the goals I wanted to achieve for myself. It was not in me to be gentle with myself.

At Christmas time, I tried, I really tried, to lose myself in the joy through Lexi's eyes. She giggled as we decorated a giant gingerbread person with gummy eyes and white frosting hair. She squealed as she waded into her enormous stocking, through books and T-shirts, to get to the mandarin orange in the toe. Not pregnant, I filled my time with other things, baking a strawberry cheesecake, a carrot cake with cream cheese icing, whipped shortbread cookies and chewy gingersnaps; decorating the house with garlands and putting up a Christmas tree as a seasonal custom. I felt compelled to fill the quiet moments and static spaces with holiday busyness.

Boxing Day was usually one of my favourite days. It was tradition for Má, Jen, and I to wade through the stores, everything half price, the thrill of the deal energizing us, as I wrestled strangers for cardigans in my size.

These were things that filled me up, warmed my spirit, and made me smile. Yet this year, there was a dimness to the holidays, a hollowness to the happy family gatherings, parties, and shopping. I thought about how much better everything would be if only I was pregnant, and I fell over the edge of grief all over again.

Although the holidays had been muted, life was at least busy this time of year, a welcomed distraction. But I knew that the next day, December 27, I would go back to work, and everything would be over, and I would be back to normal life. No pregnancy. No relief at work to look forward to, just another dreary January and deep chill of winter to get through. A frozen land, the barrenness stretched out before me. Everything was at a standstill. I was just waiting, month by month, menstrual cycle by menstrual cycle, holding my breath. The space between exhalation and inhalation stretched out before me like the horizon of the flat prairie lands—endless.

The garment I had fashioned walking with Inanna was long-gone, cut and burned clean off me. I wasn't going to look externally to collect or uncover new threads and new pieces to stitch together. I didn't know what to do next.

I hadn't written anything since my Athabasca course ended in the fall except for a few journal entries. I couldn't. Thinking about writing brought me only a sense of emptiness.

On December 27, I checked the voicemail on my cell phone from the Manitoba Writers' Guild. I should have kept the recording. I listened to it so many times. I played it for Ryan and Jen to prove to myself I wasn't hallucinating. While I was grieving and turned away from writing those last few weeks, my application was being reviewed and considered. I'd been accepted into the mentorship program.

A spark. New hope, new purpose poured into me to fill me up. Perhaps Quan Âm had heard my prayers after all. Instead of a baby, she gave me something else to focus on, to shift my attention away from obsessing over not being pregnant. Perhaps she gave me the gift I had been asking about for a longer time—an opportunity to focus on my writing.

Not a pregnancy. But it was a light through the Dark Days.

At the program meet-and-greet at the Guild's office in the Artspace Building in the Exchange District, my heart beat loudly in my ears. I wondered if anyone else could hear it. I had looked at my clothes for a long time before picking out a sheer pink short-sleeve blouse over a black tank top, grey cardigan, black pants, and high boots. Did I look like a writer and not a nine-to-five office-worker corporate type?

What if I am the oldest person there, the oldest mentee, I had asked Ryan. He paused a moment. *I don't think you'll be the oldest person there*, he responded. Ryan always told me his true opinion and not just what he thought I wanted to hear.

I wasn't the oldest person there. I was, however, the only person of colour who was a mentee, which did not surprise me. Living on the prairies, it was not uncommon to be the only person of colour in whatever situations I found myself. The room held a fairly equal balance of men and women. A few mentees were in their twenties and in university. A few mentees were like me, in their thirties and just coming to writing or coming back, to fill the space that life had opened.

When it was my turn to introduce myself to the group, I referred to the career I had spent thirteen years pursuing at the Workplace as my *day career*. "In the space I create for myself, I write fiction and nonfiction." It represented a shift in my own thinking to talk about it in that way. The words felt funny coming out of my mouth, so new and foreign, like I was attempting to speak a different language.

My mentor was a poet. She had flowing silvery white hair and eyes that saw through my exterior. Her elbows looked as sharp as her gaze. Bright red lipstick hinted at vibrancy. Before this meeting, I had bought two of her books and watched her readings on YouTube. She embodied the crone aspect of the Triple Goddess maiden, mother and crone of Wiccan traditions. She embodied the wisdom of experience, having lived through many waxing and waning moons, to pass on her knowledge to the next generation.

We sat together and ate our cookies and drank our juice. She asked a few times, "So you're not a poet?"

I shook my head. "I'm writing creative non-fiction." Her eyes widened and her forehead wrinkled. She seemed disappointed. Or perhaps just perplexed. Perhaps there had been a mix-up in the matching process.

"What do you write about?"

"My personal spiritual journey."

My mentor nodded and brought her hands together. Perhaps it wasn't a mix-up. My mentor had a degree in Religion and was a seeker herself. After that, we were in sync.

* * *

Dr. Y had given us the green light to start trying again in February. At the end of February, my period was one day late, and I was already calculating my due date, the hope more than half formed already. October would be a pretty time of year to have a baby, not too close to Lexi's third birthday or to Ryan's birthday or Christmas.

When blood stained my underwear a few hours later, I was on my phone in the bathroom, looking up implantation bleeding. The internet said that it usually looked like intermittent pink spotting. But maybe this red blood dripping into the toilet was actually implantation bleeding. The used tissues wet with my tears were crumpled on the counter. How could it be my period? How could I wait yet another month?

I was living for the future, racing toward the end of each day so I could achieve my goal, my legs tingling to run past this delay, my fingers wiggling to break this holding pattern.

Work was busy. My mentorship program was going well. Lexi was a curious and chattering toddler. Even though my life was full, as hard as I tried to focus elsewhere, my life was still measured in months, moon to moon, menstrual cycle to menstrual cycle, highlighted by the days I was fertile. I looked for signs of ovulation from vaginal discharge changing from a creamy substance to a sticky egg-white consistency, a sticky trap for the sperm.

At the beginning of March, we came back from a family vacation to Cuba and Ryan and I both fell incredibly ill. After dropping Lexi in her crib, hoping she didn't cry for us, I puked until only dry heaves came, leaving me dizzy with dehydration. I dreamt of implantation in my delirium. I prayed to Quan Âm that all this sickness didn't somehow flush out or dislodge the tiny cluster of cells that hopefully were attaching to my uterus. I prayed that the miracle of something new could be happening in the same body that was rejecting all fluids and rendered immovable due to exhaustion.

At the end of March, my period was one day late, two days late, then three days late. This was the realm of the unknown, the realm of the possible; it was too beautiful to give up. Did I want to know? How could I deal with disappointment again? If I wasn't pregnant now, and if I got pregnant next month in April, my due date would be around Christmas. Ugh. If I got pregnant in May, my due date would be January and Lexi and her sibling would be four school years apart. The baby would be one of the oldest kids in their class, did I really want that? These were the kind of thoughts weighing me down.

I felt like I had been waiting and dreaming and hoping since last June after Ryan broke his leg. To a person who loved to plan everything, this uncertainty was a hard lesson to learn. If only I could control it.

I told myself I would wait to take the pregnancy test the next morning. That night, I dreamt I took the test and it was negative. My heart dropped. I dreamt again I took the test and I didn't look at the results. I couldn't look. That night, I must have taken the pregnancy test a dozen times.

On the Sunday morning in late March when I finally took the pregnancy test, I stared at the results for one minute, two minutes, then three minutes. From the other side of the bathroom door, Ryan asked me how it was going.

Two straight pink lines.

Two wondrous pink lines, the best artwork I had ever seen.

The circular window on the right was the control, and there was a bold fuchsia line. The window on the left was the result, and there it was, a shy rose line.

I squealed. Ryan hugged me tightly and we breathed out together, the breath we had both been holding in since the miscarriage.

I took a picture of my pregnancy test. I had physical evidence this was real, this was happening. My mind had not conjured an outcome from air and wishes. Almost every day, I looked at the photo and let out a breath, feeling a prickling in my fingers and a warmth deep near my navel. I zoomed in on that photo so many times, to make sure the pink line hadn't disappeared.

* * *

I picked up the phone while still scanning an email. "Human Resources. Linda speaking."

It was a client manager wanting to discuss a few things. I made a few notes, adding to my to-do list. We talked briefly about changes to the Workplace. He expressed how he thought things will get better, how he was optimistic, and how in the next few months, things would settle down.

I picked up the worry rock on my desk, but no longer needed to rub it as often as I had a few months ago.

After a year and a half, I no longer expected to see my Old Leader emerging from my New Leader's office. The Old Workplace was comforting and warm, a soft place to land in my memory. Yet the emerging New Workplace was refreshing and interesting. I was gaining experience in my new role, I had accepted that some days would still be tough and tried not to be surprised when that happened. What did surprise me were the good days, when clients thanked me for my guidance, when I was proud of the service I provided. As I was building new relationships and new memories of the New Workplace, I discovered the strength of spirit in my colleagues and discovered the strength of spirit within myself.

Was I transforming into a new kind of employee? I loosened my grip on memories not as sharply painful as they once were. I wrapped up the past in a package and buried it in the closet, relinquishing its power to haunt me. I locked away the knowledge and skills related to the role I previously held to be used at a different time, in a different way. I focussed on and tried to refine the new knowledge and skills I needed for my current position.

I came to realize I was no longer consumed by fears of losing my job as I had been throughout the Dark Days. I no longer daydreamed almost daily about looking for a different job—working on my resume, checking the job postings. And I no longer daydreamed constantly about quitting my job and just writing.

I had dropped off the cheque to Lexi's childcare provider before coming to work to make a list of everything she had grown out of – pink wetsuit she wore in Cuba, first pair of flip-flops, her bunny pyjamas. I wanted to travel again; sacred spaces still beckoned to me. We would want a second car at some point. Writing didn't pay the bills.

I had to make a choice. The New Workplace was still a steady income with a great benefits package. The job made sense for my family and made sense for the life I wanted. I realized I needed to be grateful for this career given the realities of the labour market.

I had to make another choice. I had seen colleagues and employees and client managers go off on sick leave and stress leave, lost in uncertainty, broken under the pressure. I would not let the New Workplace take any-thing away from me in the form of stress, worry, waking up in the middle of the night paralyzed under pressure. I owed the New Workplace a full day of work, to be a professional and engaged employee. But I did not owe the New Workplace anything more than that.

I had to re-evaluate what work meant to me and what value I placed on it. I had to shift my perspective and embrace who I was now. I was no longer Moses, but rather Joseph, not the old employee, but now had the new identity that was needed. The space that the fear had once occupied was va-cant now, an opening to invite in something new, something more hopeful.

I'd experienced a year and a half of organizational change, a journey fraught with pain, losing parts of my spirit along the way. I survived the wilderness but not without scars. Not without regrets. Not without it having changed me. I had spoken and behaved in ways that were unkind, gossipy, mean-spirited, resentful, negative. I cringed reflecting on my behaviour.

I lost pieces of my integrity, pieces of myself scattered throughout the terrain of the wilderness, that would never be restored to me. Why had I devalued myself? Acted less than myself, than what I wanted to be? Emperor Lê and King Arthur felt far away. I'd been in survival mode for a long time. Forever changed. Now made anew. This was the cost, the price to pay after wandering the wilderness.

I had loved the Old Workplace.

Now that it had passed away, I would not give away my heart again.

Change is external. Change is situational. Change may be fast.

Transition is internal. Transition is psychological. Transition may be slow.

Transition involved the spirit. The mind might accept the new reality, but the spirit must embrace it for the transition to be complete.

* * *

"I have more for you," my mentor said as she pulled beautiful books from her backpack. Books by Annie Dillard. Books of mythology. Tales told long ago. She put into my hands the translated poem of Inanna's descent into the underworld.

The restaurant across the street from the University of Winnipeg served avocado and bacon on multigrain for me and Havarti cheese and ham on sourdough for her and the city's best carrot cake to split. Red wine for her and gourmet lemonade for me. This was our ritual.

We focussed on her critique of my latest work, a revision of the draft about my travels through Abu Simbel in Egypt. I was writing about experiencing a ceremony from long ago deep in the inner sanctuary of the temple.

"You were called," she said.

Serving the crone aspect of the Triple Goddess, my mentor walked with me through my own memories, to support me in writing the stories of my life. These were stories I had never even shared with Jen or Ryan. She held a torchlight to guide me on my journey. She challenged me to dig deeper, mine for the buried stuff, the gold, the glitter, to bring into the light.

I had taken online courses on and off throughout the years, whenever I felt within me the urge to pursue writing. Athabasca. Humber. I submitted assignments and received feedback by email. I was left to interpret the instructor's words myself as I hunched over my computer and anxiously opened the documents. What did they like about it? What grade did I get?

I'd never before had a writing mentor to sit and banter with, to bounce ideas off in the moment. The ebb and flow of ideas, the spark of synergy— until I experienced it, I did not realize the power of this type of connection, the nourishment it provided.

Like the fairy godmother of fairy tales, my mentor gave me just what I needed to push through the obstacles and barriers I created for myself.

Every book my mentor handed to me became a key. "This is a way in," she always said. A key to the possibilities of creation, of creativity. She revealed what it meant to sit with my creativity, to trust myself and my craft.

She was the dark of the moon, the quiet energy, the resting wisdom of time and eternity. Through her, I experienced the power necessary to bring about the sliver of waxing crescent moon, new creation, and light to begin again.

* * *

Long ago, Quan Âm lived as a peasant woman named Thị Kính in Vietnam. She was blessed with beauty and kindness. Her husband falsely accused her of trying to murder him while he slept and threw her out of the house. She disguised herself as a man and sought sanctuary in a Buddhist monastery.

A wealthy woman patron who often visited the monastery fell in love with the disguised Thị Kính and accused her of being the father of her infant. Once again, Thị Kính was cast out and became a beggar, with the child in her arms. Close to death, Thị Kính returned to the monastery, revealed she was a woman, asked for mercy for her sins, and perished.

She became the Goddess of Mercy. She is the protector of women and children. She hears the prayers of those who are suffering and saves them.

* * *

This time around, I asked for a referral to see the OB earlier, to see if that would calm my anxiety. Normally a pregnant woman in Manitoba has her first appointment at twelve weeks, after the first trimester when the chance of miscarriage decreased greatly. I went in at seven weeks, switching over to Dr. Y, the same doctor who treated me after my miscarriage. The same Dr. Y who had removed the remaining products of conception that finally allowed my uterus to heal and prepare for this new occupant. Dr. Y said everything looked normal. There was really nothing he or I could do.

Week 8 – kidney bean.

Week 9 – grape.

Week 10 – kumquat.

Week 11 – fig.

I had been here before. I remembered those sizes. The clock had started over again and I was marking off the same milestones. Other than Má, Jen, and my best friend, I didn't share my happy news with anyone. Even though I wished I had shared more widely after I miscarried, fear held me back.

I focussed on work and on my writing. I kissed Lexi before bed and sang to her. Other than doing what I was supposed to be doing physically, I did not acknowledge my pregnancy at all. In a way, I built a barrier between what I focussed on and what my body was doing. Ryan and I didn't talk about our new fetus—new Fety.

At 12 weeks – lime.

I had been here before.

I didn't exercise. I didn't go out. I went to work and came home. I hugged my daughter. I waited.

The date of the miscarriage last year was Wednesday, November 13, one day before I was twelve weeks pregnant. Now it was Wednesday, May 14, a day before I was twelve weeks pregnant. Six months to the day after my miscarriage, I heard Fety's heartbeat at Dr. Y's office. The sound on the doppler was fast and clear, like the footfalls of a racing horse. I closed my eyes and smiled.

As before, I followed all the pregnancy guidelines. I continued to take a prenatal vitamin every day and go to the gym and eat lean protein. I didn't eat soft cheeses or sushi of any kind. I did all these things I was supposed to do. Yet when I thought of Fety, I shifted my focus elsewhere. Ryan and I didn't talk about Fety. We didn't plan anything. I didn't buy anything. I did nothing to call attention to my happiness for fear it would be taken from me. This was the only way I could shield my heart and keep getting out of bed in the morning.

A week later, I was in Edmonton to attend training offered to managers and HR in the New Workplace.

"And what about you? Kids?" a client manager asked me during a health break. We had spoken on the phone many times before, but this was the first time we had met in person.

"I have a daughter, two-and-a-half years old." I thought about telling her I was pregnant with my second child. It seemed like a natural point in the conversation to bring it up. I didn't. "What about you?"

I was wearing a maternity shirt, bright pink, stretchy. I was not hiding my slight baby bump. I just wasn't announcing it widely. It was like I had forgotten how to say the words *I'm pregnant*. I didn't say it often.

I didn't say those words to anyone for three days in Edmonton, a mixed group of employees from different locations. I had never been one to make jokes about eating for two or pregnancy brain.

It wasn't until a large group of us gathered for lunch at a restaurant on the last day when someone mentioned my pregnancy directly to me.

"I was speaking with your colleague and learned you are pregnant. Congratulations," a client manager from Winnipeg said to me.

"Thank you." I didn't know what else to say.

"How far along are you?"

"Fifteen weeks." I didn't offer any more details and the conversation moved to another topic.

Perhaps talking about it would invite evil spirits or jealous sprites to me. Perhaps if I said nothing, nothing bad would happen.

I came back from Edmonton and told Ryan who said, "I don't think we need to be any more fearful than anyone else at this stage." Even with my previous pregnancy loss, after making it past the first trimester, after hearing the heartbeat, it was probably true my odds of a healthy pregnancy were the same as any other pregnant woman.

Yet I was so afraid to hope, to plan for this baby. The risk of being crushed was too great.

* * *

Subject: Invitation to Linda's reading event

   Hello Family and Friends,

   Hope you're all well.

   As some of you may or may not know, I have been involved in a mentorship program for the last five months through the Manitoba Writers' Guild. (One more step toward my goal of being a published author one day.)

   As part of the program, the Guild is hosting a wrap-up party and all participants will read a bit of their work. It is with some fear and lots of excitement that I invite you to this event – my first public reading! (Eek!)

   Thanks for your support,

   Linda

I was breathless as I hit "send." I covered my eyes and couldn't believe what I'd just done. What if no one came? Or worse, what if people came? I was risking sharing a piece of myself that had been kept private for so long.

I didn't know if immigrant parents ever encouraged their children to pursue the arts. Má thought it was fine when I wrote stories as a kid, but never believed I would make it a realistic career choice.

I had needed a practical degree and a steady income to be able to contribute financially to the family, so Má could stop working. I had needed to get Má settled in a nice neighbourhood so Jen and I bought a house in the suburbs. I had needed to attempt to repay what my mom had given to me, what she had given up for me.

So I had made a choice. I got my Bachelor of Commerce degree and a steady job right out of university. I paid my way through university with scholarship money, part-time work at the bookstore, and my sister supplemented the rest.

Then, for a while, I turned away from writing and set aside those dreams of being a published author and spending my days and nights crafting stories. I sealed away that part of myself. I believed at that time that I couldn't have it all—writing and my day career. Writing was an indulgence Má, Jen, and I could not afford.

Wearing the same stretchy pink maternity shirt I had worn in Edmonton when I could not speak about my pregnancy, I spoke a few words of introduction at the mentorship reading. "Before I start, I want to speak briefly about the program. It came at the right time in my life, when I needed something to look forward to, something to focus on. This program became a ray of light in my life."

As I began reading my own work, looking out at the crowd of my loved ones, locking eyes with Ryan, seeing Má and Jen paying close attention, looking at my mentor as she closed her eyes listening to my words, it became clear to me NOW was the time to turn back to writing. Now was the time to turn back to the dreams of my childhood and ultimately, to turn back to myself. A clarity so sharp washed over me, that I had to blink my eyes a few times.

I didn't need to remake the garment that had been worn and torn during the Dark Days. I didn't need those coverings.

The night of the reading, the moon was waning gibbous, past full moon, and now spinning toward the phase of the dark moon. I harnessed the bright beauty of the full moon, channelled that strange and dynamic power inward, to my spirit, to my core, as fuel for my creativity. I was moving toward a new phase of writing.

In my new ritual as a writing mom working full-time, the ordinary brushed up against the sacred. Ryan and I took turns with Lexi's bedtime routine. After she was in bed, I wrote. She sometimes had night terrors and after I put her back to bed, I wrote. I fell asleep exhausted. Yet I felt a sense of peace deep within, with my palm over my growing belly again. As Fety was growing, I channelled that nervous energy and poured it into my writing. The writing became the joy, calling attention away from the pregnancy. I was so tired and yet so happy. Writing became a bridge between work, the emerging New Workplace, and growing Fety, the new beginning of life. Writing was the space in-between. It was something just for me.

What I wrote during this time ignited as the first sparks of life, the emergence of essays, bits and pieces of tales that would later shift and morph into published works and chapters of this book. As life grew inside me, needing me and nourished by me, I leaned into focusing on my developing desires.

I learned to mould my words into shape, and build my scenes, my descriptions, revisit my memories, connect those memories to concepts rolling around in my head. Spirituality was always on my mind. The questions needed to be explored in words on the screen. I breathed life into my ideas, giving shape and structure to them as Fety was taking shape.

* * *

At twenty weeks, I attended my first ultrasound appointment, with sweaty palms and a rapid heartbeat. I was praying for the best, yet dreading the possibility of awful news. Walking into the room, Ryan right behind me, I was momentarily terrified the technician would tell me I was growing a monster, like a dragon or a unicorn.

The gel the technician squirted on my belly was warm, not the usual cool. "I keep the gel on the machine so the engine keeps it warm." She was not like the technician we'd had with Lexi, all business, conducting a medical test, nothing more. This technician took her time, and smiled brightly, feeling our excitement as her own.

Shifting my head further to one side to see the monitor, I held my breath.

As she pushed down on my uterus, I instantly felt the need to pee, again. I hoped this wouldn't take too long.

A real fetus, not a dragon, appeared. Head. Heart. Lungs. Two legs. Two arms.

I breathed out, my pulse steadying.

"You want to know the sex?"

When I was pregnant with Lexi, we'd been at an impasse. Ryan wanted to be surprised. I needed to know. I played my trump card. I was the one who was pregnant. If someone had to decide, it really should be me. He relented. I told him if and when we had another pregnancy, he could decide. Now, he wanted to know too.

"Look there, do you see something there, between the legs?" the technician asked. Technically, she couldn't tell us, she had to write a report and our OB would tell us at our next appointment.

I could see it in Ryan's eyes. The dream. A baby boy. A boy to take to hockey and whatever else fathers dreamt about doing with their sons.

I almost burst into tears. Not tears of relief or tears of joy, but tears of dread.

Guard your heart, I warned silently. Was I telling Ryan or was I telling myself?

I was nervous and trying not to be. My miscarriage had taken away the innocence of pregnancy. I knew what could and did go wrong. The fear was so ingrained that I was depriving myself of the deliciousness of anticipation.

When pregnant with Lexi, as time had gone on, the more I believed everything would go well. With her, I had known the risks, but they were never tangible. They were faraway possibilities, in the same way I could be hit by a bus whenever I stepped outside.

As time went on with this pregnancy, the more I dreaded something would go terribly wrong. I was caught in the web of thinking and reverse thinking and over-thinking and wishing and hoping and over-wishing and over-hoping. But then if I didn't acknowledge this pregnancy, would the universe think I was not grateful, that I did not want such a future?

If I didn't dare to hope, would my sorrow be any less if something terrible happened than if I threw my whole heart into wishing and dreaming and planning for a baby? Perhaps I thought it would, but I was tricking myself anyway.

Ever since the two pink lines appeared on the pregnancy test, I had been holding my breath, taken hostage by a dream. I'd attempted to distract myself, yet the thoughts crept in—fluctuating between consciously being positive and the opposite, thinking every little twinge was IT, the end. I tried not to "go there" and then going there, I told myself not to do that again.

I needed to make a choice. I did not want to rob myself of the joy this expectant time could bring. To embrace the unknown of the future was the hardest thing I had to do. To loosen my grip on my dread and crumple it up and throw it away became my biggest challenge. To make room for joy and anticipation. To give myself permission to wish again.

Only then did I allow myself to imagine a little boy, a baby in my arms, a brother for Lexi. Nothing could snatch it from my grasp again.

One year after the miscarriage, I was waiting anxiously for my baby boy to arrive.

When we began the journey of trying for a second child, I said I did not want another November baby, so close to Lexi's birthday and Ryan's birthday. So close to Christmas. So the universe needed to teach me a lesson. We were expecting a November baby.

Perhaps Fety would be born on November 13—exactly a year after the miscarriage. A full circle.

Breathe out. Pause. Breathe in. Start again.

A baby born after a miscarriage is known as a rainbow baby. Beauty after the storm.

Change is external. Change is situational. Change may be fast.

Transition is internal. Transition is psychological. Transition may be slow.

* * *

Quan Âm remained silent. Her silence spoke loudly.

These past two years, I had set my heart on the path toward her. I engaged in prayer and meditation, imagined her light and asked for her strength. I cried out to her at the darkest time of my life. I chose her from the land of my ancestors to guide me on my journey toward the divine feminine. She possessed the power of compassion and mercy I wanted to cultivate as my own.

I had passed through all my gates of the underworld and had figured out the secrets of spirit. Or so I had thought.

I thought I had it all figured out. But the *me* I had woven together was not up for the challenges of life. I thought all I needed to do was examine spirit, take a magnifying glass to it, turn it inside out, explore it through books and research, contemplate and reflect upon it. Once I studied it, I would have everything I needed. I then stitched the bits and pieces of myself from threads I collected all over the world and from my own life and fashioned a garment to help me in the world.

After these past two years, I recognized the garment was not strong enough to weather the Dark Days. It lay in tatters before me. The cost was high for such a revelation.

I reacted to the changes that were happening around me. I mourned. I adapted. I re-imagined. As the passive object being acted upon, I was looking outside myself for someone to save me. Má. Jen. Ryan. Lexi. And Quan Âm. I had placed my faith in something other than myself.

I waited for any signs from Quan Âm. The profound silence was my sign.

What would happen if I no longer waited? If I could be the active energy? What would happen if I placed my faith in myself? Perhaps that would be the next chapter of my journey to explore.

In the wilderness, I'd left some things behind. It was challenging to not think about what could have been. What if I'd had a six-month baby now instead of a swollen belly. If I had lost my job and needed to decide what to do with the rest of my career life. If I'd allowed the Dark Days of everything that was happening at the time to consume me, turn my passion into bitterness, turn my nostalgia into a sense of loss, to let the grief overtake me. If I'd never turned back to writing.

I left those possibilities behind in the silver light of the wilderness. I left behind the reflected silver light of the moon through her phases, illuminating all my collected stones and rocks.

I envisioned the promised land as starlight in the darkness. Against the black backdrop encircling me, tiny glowing points appeared, a million suns radiating light and warmth. This was not reflected light but direct light. Each star represented a possibility, a chance, a future. New energy and new hope. I breathed out and breathed in and I began to expand, stretching and reaching, dissolving and diffusing until the stars became me, and I became the starlight. As I had been formed by the stardust of the universe, I returned to the dust of the stars. The spark within me caught fire.

PART III
PRACTISING SPIRIT

Seven: Sacred Mind

EMERGING FROM THE WILDERNESS, I am back where I started, bits and pieces of myself, without binding material. To move forward, I turn and gaze backward, to reflect on where I began. With all the layers burned away, I sink down, and I rediscover my roots. The foundation, the bedrock, is intact. If my roots are not strong, I can not grow. I look to Buddhism again, exploring possibilities. I had previously tried to amplify my connection to Quan Âm but I can no longer wait for the divine to come to me. I want to move, no longer content to stay still.

I seek a different way to connect to spirit, to seek the sacred in my daily life. I begin to meditate, putting an aspect of Buddhism into practice. I choose to meditate by focussing on a mandala, having always been fascinated by its construction and its representation of the impermanence of life. When I was a teenager, Tibetan monks spent months at the Winnipeg public library creating a sand mandala. I remember being awestruck by TV clips showcasing monks creating designs with coloured sand; they had steady hands and calm expressions as they bent over their work. When it was completed, they swept the masterpiece away.

Mandala literally translates as "circle" in Sanskrit. This is the language of ancient India, the language of Hinduism and of Buddhism as Buddhism spread across Asia and came to Vietnam. In Buddhist iconography, the complete universe is represented within the mandala. I first use a familiar mandala as a tool for visualization. The mandala of Avalokiteshvara, a prominent figure in Mahayana Buddhism, is found in *The Encyclopedia of Eastern Mythology*, which I bought many years ago while working as a bookseller at Smithbooks. I have poured over its pages countless times, spellbound by the many tales. Avalokiteshvara the bodhisattva – a future Buddha—of compassion. It's always fascinated me that over hundreds of years, as Buddhism travelled from India to China to Vietnam, HE evolved into SHE, none other than Quan Âm, Goddess of Mercy. This mandala is a complex scene of circles within squares within circles. Its vibrant colours come from the natural world, earthly pigments of budding spring and hues of the sky on a clear day. Human figures float inside and outside the mandala, on the grass, above the ground, in flowing robes, floating on lotus blossoms, their gazes all focussed on the deity in the centre.

Travelling the Mandala

Another way I use a mandala for meditation is to go on an internal journey starting from the outside travelling into the centre. I close my eyes and build my own mandala in my mind in its most basic form: an outer ring, an inner temple, and inside the centre, a deity. As I make the journey, I am surprised and curious to discover that the males I love most inhabit the mandala of my mind. As I encounter each of them, I am forced to encounter elements of my own life – dreams, disappointments, fears, and joys.

The Outer Ring

As I visualize the outer ring, I am greeted by a wall of flame that encircles the entire mandala, a common element of Buddhist mandalas. This signifies the outer edge of the universe. Outside, in the darkness and nothingness, a force pulls at me, wanting to engulf me in the absence of light. This protective ring of fire may burn away the impurities of a seeker who dares to breach it. Like the Goddess Inanna at the first gate of the underworld, I face another journey inward.

Breathing in, I move through. The flames caress my cheeks and singe the ends of my hair. Yet there is no scent and there is no sound. This is no earthly fire. I hesitate, in-between; is this really a place I want to enter? This flame consumes energy and casts energy. Red embers spark, orange tendrils lick, and yellow tips dance around me. What is the cost to me for crossing into this realm and when will payment be due, I wonder.

I breathe out and emerge on the other side, on the inside. I am tired already from my efforts yet relieved I have made it this far.

Ba is here.

He is a shadow in the light. A presence without form or substance. He is an outline shimmering at the edges, between what is and what was, what is lived and what is remembered.

We were supposed to have lived the good life. We left Vietnam after the war so Ba could find his fortune in the new world, open a business, and work deep into the night. All so that Jen and I could live without the cares of the world, not understanding the sacrifices and hardships of our immigrant parents. We were supposed to have grown up in the suburbs of the centre of the universe, Toronto, having moved there briefly after first starting out in Winnipeg. We were supposed to take ballet and play soccer, and follow our own passions, trying out job after job, chasing our bliss, secure in Ba and Má's ability to support and shelter us from the rougher edges of life.

Instead, our lives turned in a different direction. After Ba died, Má moved us back to be with family in Winnipeg, to a rented apartment on Beverley Street, a green brick building with three flights of stairs where we all slept in the one bedroom, in a neighbourhood where the sound of police sirens was common. The three of us lived the classic immigrant tale of a single mother working for minimum wage, Má sewed our clothes herself from discounted rolls from the bulk fabric store. I grew up excited for the Winnipeg Cheer Board's hamper of food and toys a few days before Christmas. Personally witnessing the hardships, living the sacrifices, and knowing that my life wasn't just about me was how I grew up.

If my life's story had been fiction, this would serve as the pivotal moment in the protagonist's life. I could not have made up a more crucial plot point for my real life. It became the defining moment for me. I grew up without a father, without a male role model, without someone to balance Má's influence. This is the point in my story to which I will always circle back. To me, this defines my identity and it defines the rest of my story.

I always wonder how my life would be different had Ba lived. Would we have moved from Toronto? Would I be in a different life? Career? Be with a different life partner? Would I feel more carefree? A sliver of sorrow is tucked in the corner of my heart as I ask these "what ifs."

I do not remember much of Ba when he was alive. His brown aviator sunglasses on the chipped laminate dresser. Watching an old VHS tape of home movies, sitting next to each other on a brown fabric couch and laughing. I enjoyed hearing the raspy quality of his voice, scratchy yet warm. He used to take me to school on the bus and sit next to me; when I once closed my eyes and dropped my mittens, he wrapped his hands around mine as a barrier against the chill. He took me to Gordon Bell High School where he worked as a teacher's aide, and I buried my face in his tickly sweater-vest, nervous around all the big kids.

Ba's ashes are still on the altar at my family's house. Má still pours tea for him every morning. We share meals with him on the anniversaries of his passing. The plastic around the golden urn has never been disturbed; it is a weight on the altar and in the house. His image, suspended in time, looks down on me behind glass, the black and white headshot from his twenties. It's not the same man I grew up with, I didn't know this man from the portrait. Yet when I think of my father, I always think of the black and white image, as that is the Ba I have lived with the longest.

I do remember his shadow form. At the tea ceremony on my wedding day, my Chú Năm, the eldest brother on my dad's side of the family, lit incense at Ba's altar, and said a few prayers. Ryan and I stood in front of the altar and bowed our heads. Ryan was dressed in a blue traditional áo dài. I was wearing a traditional áo dài too, bright pink overlying a pale-yellow tunic and pants. I visualized Ba taking my hand and threading it through his arm, patting it with his other hand, to calm my nerves. This wasn't Ba in the physical sense. I was not trying to add layers to my wedding day by thinking of what he was in this life, of skin and bone, words and laughter, what he wore against his skin, and laced up on his feet, glasses framing his face.

All I know was that I felt him with me on my wedding day, though not in the flesh. It was not empty space. He filled the space around the edges and between the other guests. He was the spark and the crackle along those edges. He drank the tea that we cúnged to him and we served to our families during the tea ceremony. We received his well wishes and prayers for a happy life and good fortune. He stood next to Má as we divided the gifts that the groom's family brought over—tea, fruit, cake—and he travelled with us to our new home. He glided beside Má as she walked me down the aisle in my white wedding dress, embracing me as she embraced me, eyes tearing during the toasts, and laughing when we played the wedding games at the reception. On a day so filled with love and light, I felt both his absence and his presence.

That sliver of sorrow in my heart is wrapped in the bindings of sharing my life with Ba after his passing. Those bindings soothe the ache.

Even after having passed into the realm of the spirits, he is an overarching presence, silken whispers along the wind. He is a shadow hiding in the light itself, through the veil, a constant presence. A hum in my mind, inside and outside, reminds me of Ba. I am not recreating the man from this life but continuing my relationship with him in his current form.

Trưng Trắc had opened the gates to the spirit world for me when I was growing up. I found my connection to those who have passed beyond this life.

And Ba is here, in the mandala of my mind. In the form he now possesses, he is a ring of fire surrounding me, protecting me. I feel blessed he is here with me.

The Four-Sided Temple

As I meditate, I keep travelling inward. Dawn breaks over the horizon, the sky a shy pink dissolving into a deep fuchsia. I hear the chirping of birds. The scents of lavender and sandalwood tickle my nose. At the back of my throat, I taste honey carried on the wind.

The temple is square shaped. In the middle of each side of the square is a T-shaped gate. The gates represent the four corners of the earth and also the four boundless thoughts of Buddhism—compassion, loving-kindness, sympathy, and equanimity. I begin at one gate and move around the square clockwise, hesitant at first, then gaining momentum as I turn the 90 degrees to get to another gate, like I'm being pushed along by the cool air until I am back to where I started at the first gate. I feel more comfortable in this space than at the outer ring. There is familiarity and memory in this movement.

I slip past the gate, entering the temple.

Ryan is here.

Unlike Ba, Ryan is well defined in shape and form. He has edges where space ends and he begins. He is the male I've lived with for the longest period of time. Aside from male cousins and uncles, he is the man I've known the longest. I walk my journey through life, and he walks alongside me. He is my companion in sacred spaces, my co-parent, my life partner. My spirit's match. Everything in the world is in him.

On the cusp of the transition from high school to university, my dream was to major in English and Religion. Instead, I chose business school. It was a practical degree, fulfilling an immigrant parent's dream. Had my life been different, had I not moved back to Winnipeg from Toronto, had I not chosen the University of Manitoba, had I not chosen the Asper School of Business, Ryan and I would not have been in the same classes, would not have noticed each other, he would not have asked me for my phone number in the computer lab on the pretense of discussing an assignment for Management Information Systems and we would not have gone to see *Vanilla Sky* at Polo Park Theatres on our first date, holding hands walking to the car.

I wonder if I had gone to business school to meet Ryan.

"Was that a leg?" Ryan asked as we watched the movie *Love Actually*, again. He put his palm over my swollen belly.

"I think that was an elbow," I grunted, jabbed from the inside again. I pulled the blanket over my shoulders, settling deeper into the couch.

Our son was two days overdue and I wondered if he was too comfortable. Frosty breath and frigid winds had forced us indoors. The snow was crumbly and dusty like powder, soft, not the sticky stuff to roll into a snowperson or snowballs. The city was draped in white; the snow would remain until the spring thaw. The snow would usher in my baby and wrap around him like a blanket through his first Manitoba winter.

Lexi had come roaring into the world almost two weeks before her due date—she couldn't wait to get out and be with us. That is still true of her. She always wants to be around people.

Unlike her, this little guy was taking his own time. He was doing life on his own terms, which I suspected would be his nature.

From deep within, I felt pressure, a deep squeeze, and rippling pain.

We watched the whole movie, munching on salt-and-vinegar chips, as I began my labour.

Eleven hours later, at the Women's Hospital at The Health Sciences Centre, I was transitioning from the second stage of labour to the third stage without any pain medication. Natural labour and delivery were still my goals. Ryan was on my right, calm, and Má, the worry obvious on her face, on my left. The room was quiet except for the buzzing of my fetal monitor and the shuffling feet of the two nurses.

Weeks earlier, I gave Ryan strict instructions on how to coach me through this labour. "Don't ask me how I'm doing. Don't ask questions. Be strong."

With Lexi's delivery, also without pain medication, Ryan had kept asking me how I was doing. I found this annoying in the moment; how do you think I'm doing?

I breathed through a couple major contractions, one wave after another. I cried and moaned, bunching my hands into the bedding. Contractions were threatening to pull me under the surface.

Another contraction hit, untethered me.

My eyes shut to ward off the pain and other sensations, the fear and the doubt of new birth. I knew the pain. I remembered the pain. I knew the risks. Could I tap out now?

I turned to Ryan. "I don't think I want to do this anymore."

"You can do it." His voice in the darkness demanded my participation. The contractions were coming whether I wanted them or not.

"You can do it." I heard Ryan's voice, connected to so many warm memories. His voice was full of confidence in me. I could tap into his strength as he breathed each breath with me, an invisible rope tying us together, binding us in this work, in this hard work.

Sweat collected on my brow. Out of nowhere, I felt the shift and the nurse could see it on my face. I was bearing down. Feeling hot and cold all over, I knew it was time to push. The doctor appeared, blonde and business-like, a tall woman with strong broad shoulders.

I shut my eyes again.

I was close. I had to concentrate on our fetus. I needed to take care of him.

Ryan was there for me, to take care of me, to do what he could so I had the strength and the endurance to do what I needed to do. He was solid and completely present, flesh and muscles, breath and voice. Standing straight like a tree with deep roots, unmovable, he was here with me.

I could detach, as I needed to, from the pain, and tie myself to him, completely confident that his dependability and strength would not fail me. I could not break as he would not break. He was the structure around me.

"You did it!" His voice brought me back from where I had meandered.

I opened my eyes to see a beautiful brightness in his eyes as we kissed.

The nurse laid our son on my chest.

Ryan is the structure as the four-sided temple gives the mandala structure. He is the form of my life. Within the outline he defines, I find safety in the familiar, security in the stability he provides. He anchors me to the world. He is my reference point, my starting point for my goals and dreams and the person I return to, I circle back to him. I choose him, everyday. I am grateful he is here with me.

The deity

In the mandala of my mind, I continue to travel inward. Deeper into the temple, the vibrant multi-coloured, multi-textured, multi-faceted world merges into white light and white sound, smooth and soft. The wonderfully distinct fragments focus into a singular point. White light, as if passed through a prism, breaks in the spectrum of the rainbow, and then comes back together, streaming into the centre as white light again, pouring energy inward toward a focal point in the centre.

I move inward. I am now calm and confident, after gathering strength being with Ba at the outer ring and with Ryan at the four-sided temple, eager to see what comes next.

At the centre of the temple, at the centre of the mandala, at the centre of universe, presides the deity. It could be a Buddha—one who has attained enlightenment—or a bodhisattva—a future Buddha who has delayed entering nirvana in order to help others reach that goal. Beams of light encircle the deity, radiating outward.

I reach the centre.

Evan is here.

My son. I finally meet him. He is where energy is focussed and where love is concentrated. The new light. He is the one we prayed for after my miscarriage of the one that never came. Brightness and air, happiness and light, he is my rainbow baby.

For two years, I have been waiting for him, counting from the moment Ryan and I made the decision to try for a second child, through the initial period trying to conceive, to praying to Quan Âm in Hà Nội at Chùa Một Cột, to being elated in pregnancy, to the devastation of the miscarriage, to the grieving, to the period of trying to conceive again, to the cautious optimism of being pregnant again, and to the deep fear of being pregnant again.

As the nurse laid him on my chest, breath to breath, skin to skin, I wondered, was he real? Finally fetus to baby? Is he actually bone and blood or did I fashion him from dreams and desperate wishing? He embodied the melding of will and action in new life. He slept on my chest that night, so used to hearing my heartbeat from the inside of my body, to regulate his own breathing, to smell my familiar scent. A feeling of contentment, of complete rightness settled over us both. I held him tight, needing to ensure I was more than just dreaming.

Evan didn't open his eyes for the first twenty-four hours of his life. He would do things on his own terms, on his own timeline, I was sure of it. He needed time to adjust to being born. Perhaps he would always need a pause to be able to change. For the first day of his life, his eyes still shut, he cried when hungry and shifted and squirmed through his swaddling, tiny tentacles through the cotton casing, that was how we knew he was awake. Almost exactly one day after he was born, he opened one eye, just a quick peek, a test, just to try it out, and then the second eye. I had him lying on my thighs, my knees bent, facing me. His green striped sleeper was almost too small for him already. He looked at me and I looked at him. Deep liquid pools for eyes. Almost too big for his face. He reflected my love for him back at me.

My son is light and air, changing over the months, the future in his eyes. Chubby cheeks, skin clear and bright. True to his middle name Hải, meaning ocean, or vastness, in Vietnamese, he is an infinite expanse of love and happiness.

I always think of him in comparison to what Lexi was like. He is a watchful and curious infant. Content sitting in his swing or lying down on his activity mat, kicking his legs and waving his arms, watching me as I move around the family room. When I hold him, he burrows his head within the nook of my armpit, wriggling his tiny body, his nose and mouth pressed flat against the folds of my skin, then sighs and sleeps. His breathing mimics my breath or does my breath adjust to his breath?

One day, at seven months old, on the floor in the family room, he sits upright on the rug playing with his wooden toy with wire lines and wooden shapes. Sitting almost cross-legged, the soles of his feet almost touch, his chubby legs exposed in his onesie, a roll of fat around his thighs and around his ankles. His onesie is a deep shade of blue, rimmed with light blue at the collar. Evan looks at me with a heartfelt grin, his tiny pearl-like bottom teeth exposed through open lips. His arms down at his sides, fingers curled inward, making loose fists.

As my daughter would later say, I wrote this memory in my head. My baby boy sitting and smiling like a bodhisattva, finding joy in the simple pleasure of learning and playing. I see in his eyes the boy, the teenager, the man. I see love in his eyes as he looks at me looking at him. I see my love reflected in his eyes, love reflecting back and forth, so on and so on, like two mirrors posed in front of each other, creating a never-ending image.

With Evan, I try very hard to let go of my expectations for motherhood. He is an entirely different entity from my daughter, I must remind myself. I learn from him and his cues. I parent the child I have and not the child I thought I wanted. I have the child I was meant to have, not the pregnancy I lost. Evan is the spark that caught fire.

As the deity at the centre, he embodies excitement for the future, bright and beautiful. I see the divine within him, the same as within me. As with Lexi who called me back to the world after travelling to the underworld with Inanna, Evan is my personal sacred. The light within him burns brightly and helps me to recognize the light within me, breath to breath, blood calling to blood, love responding to love. My heart barely contains the bliss I feel having him here with me.

* * *

I am surprised my dad, my life partner, and my son inhabit the mandala of my mind. I wonder why they are there. These are the males I love most in the world, but I wonder if their presence signifies reasons beyond love.

I peer beyond my loved ones into eternity to seek the answers, time and the timeless, the beginning and the ending and the beginning again. I interpret each manifestation as a facet of my own mind.

Ba—my origin story. I know the past is always with me.

Ryan—how to be a hero in my own story. I know I build my own life's structure.

Evan—my legacy and the potential for the future. I know I look forward to the journey ahead, to the possibilities.

These are the threads of my life that were always here. I did not need to seek them. I always had them.

The past. The present. The future.

I envision a circular journey—from the past, informing the present, moving into the future, reflecting on the past, and again. Completing the cycle, where I return is where I begin again. I open my eyes and I complete my practice.

Travelling the Circle

Mandalas—now referring to any geometric design or symmetrical pattern—have moved outside the realm of institutional religions of Hinduism and Buddhism. In bookstores, there are mandala colouring books. People paint mandalas on rocks. There are mandala prints for shirts and tablecloths.

As mandalas are being explored more widely, I am also exploring them in different ways. After having visualized through a mandala, I deepen my meditation practice by engaging differently with a mandala. I want to be the starting point for my own spark of spirit. As I create my own mandala, the act of creation helps me focus, and as I focus, I write, and as I write, I create. I work my way through the circle of my own creativity.

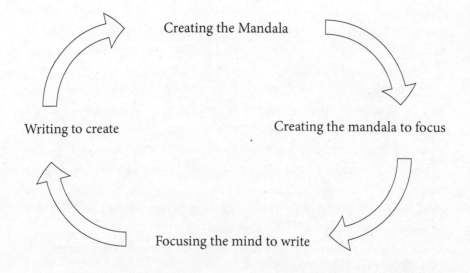

Creating the Mandala

Writing to create

Creating the mandala to focus

Focusing the mind to write

Creating the Mandala

After Evan was born, I began to colour in mandalas that were already drawn. The pencil crayon was hard in my hands, it made an indent in the index finger of my left hand, irritating me as I coloured. The medium was not the right one. Next, I coloured in mandalas with acrylic paint and a paintbrush. Still not quite right, but I was getting closer to the sensation I sought.

I chafed at the idea of having to choose a design. What would fit? What would match what I am thinking? How would I find meaning in the design? So I began to draw my own mandalas.

A Friday night at home was a rare opportunity to invite stillness. Lexi and Evan were sleeping upstairs. When I left their rooms, she was on her side nestled between two beloved teddy bears, and he was on his tummy, his chewed-up stuffed moose jammed in the crook of his neck. I was filled with gratitude watching their little chests rise and fall with their breaths. The kitchen was tidy and Ryan was at hockey. I could start laundry, write the grocery list, look at colours for vinyl siding for the house, answer emails about playdates and kids' activities, finally start planning the big birthday party for Má, see what I'd been missing on Facebook, or attend to numerous other tasks.

Instead of any of those productive tasks, I chose to focus inward, and on myself. I chose to reclaim my identity outside of mother, doer-for-others, perpetuating the myth of the Super Mom. I exhaled the tension I was holding inside. It had been a busy day, a hectic week, in a full life.

I had drawn my first mandala a few weeks ago completely free-hand. This time, I wanted a little more structure to anchor the image. Standard black construction paper from Lexi's art supply and the shimmery silver Sharpie that loved ones used to write well wishes in our guest book at our wedding ten years ago were my tools. In the centre of the page, I traced two circles, the inner one from the ring of a Scotch tape holder, the outer one the ring from a spool of green painter's tape from the junk drawer. As I drew the circle, the marker ran smoothly around the coarse paper, coming back to meet its beginning.

While CNN background noise tethered me to the outside world, I de-scended into myself. I tapped into my meditation practice of travelling the mandala to attempt to make the rest of the world fall away.

Starting at the inner circle, I drew a petal at the top, and at the bottom, as similar in size and shape as I could. A petal on the left, and its mirror form on the right. My four quadrants—four directions, the four winds, the four elements gave my universe and my sphere of influence shape.

I drew a petal in-between the top petal and the left petal, its mirror image in-between the bottom petal and the right petal. And on and on. Balance and symmetry. I drew a line from between each petal outward, connecting the inner ring to the outer ring. I was defining my space until I had eight segments of equal size and shape. My mind was defining my life's priorities, areas to bring my energy to: my health, my life partner, my kids, my writing and so on.

Outside the outer ring, there was nothing. So then everything was possi-ble. I found the mid-point of each segment and placed a dot half the height of the length of a segment. Next, I drew a curved line from the segment line to a dot, and a line from the other side. This formed a triangle and soon I had eight triangles around the segments. In between each triangle, I placed a dot and drew curved lines to the dot. And on and on. I searched for the next possibility, making the new connection. I built out from the centre. As I continued outward, the forms and shapes became crooked and sloppy, much more so than the forms closer to the centre. As in life, as I moved further and further away from my sphere of influence, the less control I had, and the more likely things went awry.

The mandala was floating in the abyss, not anchored to anything. There needed to be something more. To hold everything together, I traced one more circle around everything using a white Ikea dinner plate. It held every-thing in. Just like life, a boundary line was needed. On the inside, there was organized chaos. This rebalanced the whole of it and pulled the focus inward.

I had built my universe, a microcosm of my world. I went back inside and filled in the negative space with dots and spirals. I drew a spiral inside the innermost circle. For the spiral, starting as a dot, I drew a curve circling further and further away. Sacred to the Great Goddess, spirals are prevalent in nature: nautilus shells, waves, spinning galaxies with curved arms embracing darkest night, devoid of light. Stardust floats in the heavens, falling to earth to become the building material of new life and spirit.

Nothing existed except for the next line I drew, the next connection I made. This was meditation in practice, an intentional focus on the present moment. Clarity of purpose. Created line by line, from the simple execution of curved lines and straight lines, a complicated cohesive picture formed.

Mandala in life. Life in mandala.

I breathed in and resurfaced to the outer world.

I blinked and realized Ryan was already home from hockey, sitting beside me on the couch watching TV. I hadn't noticed when he came home. It was bright in the family room. I was thirsty, and my feet were cold, despite wearing my fuzzy pink-striped socks.

I looked at my mind's creation. This mandala was not Buddhist in form. It was entirely mine. In this moment, my mind was mine.

Creating the mandala to focus the mind

Mind clutter is my daily adversary. Even when my body is resting, my mind is still active—what do I need to do next? What's coming up? And my most feared question—what am I missing? I feel I am always moving from one thing to another, not appreciating what is happening right now.

Brushing my teeth, I'm fixated on my upcoming day at work, already projecting myself into my workstation, on the phone and answering emails as quickly as I can. I catch myself. I bring to mind the spiral at the centre of the mandala I drew. I breathe out and I taste the peppermint in my mouth, the bristles along my teeth. In the space between breaths, I stand tall and stretch my back, grateful that I have no aches and pains through my body today.

Sitting at my workstation, I'm writing a to-do list for the weekend: Birthday gift for Lexi for her friend's party, check if the kids have outgrown their bathing suits before swimming classes start, ask Ryan if he is researching siding companies. I catch myself. With my finger, I draw a circle on my desk, a square inside the circle, and a triangle inside the square—my simple form of a mandala. Then I do it again. I see the shapes on the surface of the desk as if there are glowing with invisible ink. I turn back to my screen and finish the email I am composing and hit "send." I have a dozen emails and documents and websites open to try to accomplish a dozen tasks at once. Instead of this game of task-switching, I choose one task and finish it to the point I can today. Then I move on to another task. The sense of accomplishment washes over me.

Having a dinner of leftovers with Ryan, Lexi, and Evan, I wish I could speed up the evening, already fast forwarding through lunch making, play time, bath, book, and bedtime, so I might have time to myself. Then I catch myself. I bring myself back to the present and walk to the hallway to gaze at my mandala taped to the wall where we display family artwork. Breathe in. I walk back to the kitchen and kiss my daughter, and my son, and my husband, thankful we are all here together for this meal. I savour the food in my mouth and smile, grateful for the simplicity and the warmth of this moment, so ordinary and yet so wondrous.

In creating the mandala, I remind myself to focus on the present, to be mindful, and not go from one moment to the next and to the next. I try not to wander, or if I do, come back from wandering as swiftly as possible. In the middle of the busy, I create stillness. I attempt to stop giving away pieces of myself to everyone and everything else.

The practice of creating a mandala has revealed to me what it feels like to be completely immersed in the activity of the moment. More bits and pieces of myself are revealed to me. They had always been there but now they are visible to me.

Focusing the mind to write

I focus inward. I carve out this space for myself. Make peppermint tea. Sit down at my desk. Turn on my beautiful purple laptop. Sigh. I stare beyond the laptop, not looking at what is in front of me. I don't type a single word yet.

My mind is a sandstorm of ideas, words, themes, images, and feelings. Dust swirling around me, first a gentle breeze, then accelerating into a substantial gust. Glittering sand encircles me and I attempt to grasp a few grains to bind together in a semblance of connected ideas and thoughts.

To formulate and to design. To write the words in my head. To conjure the forms of the essays and chapters. Before I even commit any words to the screen, watching the blink of the cursor, in my mind the storm is active, gold glitter and silver sparkle dancing on the wind in my mind space. This is the act of creation. Before anything is written down, typed out, or verbalized, this is where it all begins.

The practice of meditation helps my mind generate the mind storm. Whether or not inspiration hits, I must focus on the present and must do the work. The racing of my heart, the smile, and the glow perhaps others can see. My body is here, yet I am inside my own mind. My mind is firing in all directions, lighting up all the pathways, spots of brightness.

I dive deep, slipping in between the realms of the mundane and the sacred, between the ordinary and the bliss, between the basic needs as a human and the divine connection to the universe. I seek to know the unknowable in finding the divine within me. When I resurface to the ordinary world, I need to blink my eyes a few times to reorient myself.

The practice of meditation is what I attempt to bring to my writing. The creativity that is sparked through drawing mandalas, I attempt to harness through my words. I always had this power that I am only uncovering now.

Writing to create and complete the circle

I pour the creativity I generate through my writing into the creation of a mandala. I no longer feel the compulsion to create on paper. I create in my mind. I create the mandala, which leads me to focus my mind, which leads me to write, which leads me to create the mandala and this brings me back to the beginning. I complete my journey. Round and round and round. The passage of the day. The cycles of the moon. The seasons. The passage of the year, Tết again, Christmas again. I am finding my own path through my circle within the universal circle.

I am shifting my energy from being passive to being active. I had been waiting for Quan Âm to shine her light on me. Her image has faded in my mind. I no longer wear her necklace, the necklace I had grasped when the Dark Days came. I had been waiting for things to happen to me.

Now, I choose to be less passive. I choose to be active.

That is what I have gained from meditation. I begin to understand my own mind. And perhaps I find the spark of the divine mind, perhaps I find a closer connection to spirit, beyond the realm of human consciousness. I now accept that I am bits and pieces. I do not need to collect more threads or to stitch myself together.

Travelling the mandala, I start at the outside and work my way in. Creating my own mandala, I start at the centre and work my way out. Energy moving inward and energy moving outward, I complete my practice.

Active meditation has revealed for me I need to move. A body at rest will remain at rest unless acted upon by an unbalanced force. Inertia is what resists motion. The unbalanced force in my case is the energy I create within myself, my spark that caught fire, and I transform that energy into dynamic energy to be able to use my hands and use my voice. I transform thought to movement. That movement ripples through my body and out my hands to my life and to the universe. As I move, I move the air around me, the space around me, my life itself.

Eight: Sacred Hands

I PLACE MY HANDS TOGETHER in front of my heart, palms and fingers touching, pointed upward. I do this at the end of every yoga class. *The goodness within me bows to the goodness within you.* I am performing a mudra when I hold my hands this way. This is the namaskara mudra—gesture of greeting, prayer, and adoration. As I continue to explore the elements of Buddhism, such as mandala, I also focus on the practice of mudra to invite spirit into my life in a more active way.

In Sanskrit, the sacred language of Buddhism, mudra means gesture, mark, seal. In Buddhist iconography, a mudra is a formal hand gesture, a statement without words. The hands of a Buddha or a bodhisattva perform a specific mudra, symbolic of her or his attributes. It is a spiritual gesture.

I recognized this spiritual gesture at the Buddhist temple. Twenty-five years after I was at Chùa Hải Hội on Burrows Avenue for Vietnamese school, I found myself at the chùa's new location on Dufferin Avenue. As I do not consider myself a Buddhist, I had stayed away from the temple. It was by chance that I was here as an adult with my extended family.

In its outdoor courtyard, Quan Âm stood almost ten feet tall in flowing robes. The statue was made of white marble. She held her hands in the same position as when I had seen her in Vietnam so many years ago. Her right hand was bent at the elbow in front of her, palm facing the left side, thumb and ring finger touching, all other fingers pointed to the sky. Her left hand poured the elixir of life from her vase.

When I tried to mimic her hand gesture, it was awkward at first. It was not natural bringing my thumb and fourth finger together, not like touching my thumb to my index finger. I had to consciously work at it. My index finger fell backward and away; my middle finger stayed parallel with my palm. My index and middle fingers created a V shape, like I was giving the sign for victory. My pinkie finger did not know what to do, hanging out there on the end by itself. My attempt did not look the same as Quan Âm's gesture. It was as if Quan Âm had no bones or sinew or tendons in her hands to tie one thing to another, so all her fingers could point straight up. If I concentrated on lifting one of my fingers, the other fingers shifted. I also tried changing the shape I was making with my thumb and ring finger. If I straightened my ring finger, the gesture looked like the head of a jackal with a long pointed nose. If I retracted my fingers to open the space to form more of a circle, I relaxed the tension on my other fingers to get them to straighten. But it was not relaxing, instead puzzling. I was holding my fingers straight up and pressing toward each other at the same time. I was pressing down my ring finger and pressing my thumb up. It took a great amount of effort to hold my hand like this. After a couple of minutes, my hand cramped and I had to release the position.

Perhaps that was the point. What seemed simple and easily performed was actually difficult to maintain. Perhaps Quan Âm had to practise that pose for many moons for it to look that easy. That was the way of so many things in life, I was discovering.

The practice of mandala helped me to channel my mind's energy. I wonder what the practice of mudra would reveal to me. As I begin to move my hands through space, they discover the invisible threads that I find already surrounding me, smooth and strong. As my hands move, I appreciate the power my hands wield and the meaning they carry. I see this meaning in my daily life.

My Family's Mudras

As I open myself up to doing mudra, I sense mudras being performed by females close to me. Each of the women I love most—my mom, my sister, and my daughter (woman-to-be)—uses her hands to express herself. Each of their styles brings to my mind a specific Buddhist mudra.

Each of their mudras evoke lessons I have learned through them, whether intentional or not. These lessons uncover fragments of strength and perseverance, of frustration and fury, of loss and disappointment, and ultimately, make up fragments of my life. Their hands, their actions, break the stillness of the world, and I stand in the path of the resulting rippling wave. As I pull on the threads of their teachings, more of myself comes to the surface and expands, pieces stretching toward each other.

The four of us create a diamond. Má is at the top point, Jen and I are the two sides, and Lexi is the bottom point. The diamond shape connects me to the mandala in my mind. Inside the mandala, there is a sacred space, a place of balance. Ba, Ryan, and Evan are there already in the mandala. Now I see how the females I love most, and I, also exist in this sacred space.

My Mom's Hands

The mudra for Má would be the varada mudra—gesture of the fulfillment of all wishes, the gesture of charity. The arm extends all the way down with the palm facing outward and pointing down, all fingers extended.

Má's hands are cracked and red, raw. She has thick knuckles which are puffy, bloated with fluid underneath the skin, and her hands are dotted with spots of irritation. To wash dishes, she wears surgical gloves, with talcum powder lingering on her cotton T-shirts sparkling in the sunlight. The strength in her grip gives way when she feels a spasm between her thumb and other fingers and she often drops a rice bowl that clinks against the metal sink, a hollow sound.

When she was a teacher in Vietnam, she stood at the front of the classroom at a chalkboard, dressed in a flowy blouse, pencil skirt, and low heels. She waved her hands at students in uniforms to emphasize the pronunciation of words causing chalk to dust her cotton skirts in the humid air.

When she was a newly landed immigrant in Canada, she operated a sewing machine, her eyes glassy, and ran line after line, stitch in and stitch out, inhaling the fabric dust floating around. Against the constant hum of the machines, hour after hour for years, her foot cramped as it hovered over the pedals and her hands ached holding the same position. Má was forced to undergo surgery in both her wrists due to repetitive strain injury, the tendons twisted and tired.

When she was a wife, mother and widow, Má cooked food from her homeland. She washed jasmine rice, rolled spring rolls, stewed eggs, and stir-fried gai lan. She sliced beef for phở, paper thin pieces of tenderloin she layered on top of rice noodles that cooked in the boiling broth she poured over the food. She served more than just food and nourished more than just our tummies.

As a child, I used to watch her make different kinds of rice cakes. Chè xôi nước, glutinous rice balls in a ginger syrup, was one of my favourites. I wrapped myself in a blanket and laid my head on a pillow on the kitchen floor.

Má stood at the counter, shifting on her slippers, kneading the glistening white dough in a metal bowl. She would pull off a ping-pong ball-sized chunk and flatten it into a circular disc. In the middle she'd place a smaller ball of yellow mung bean that she had prepared earlier, and begin folding the dough over the mung bean, twirling and twisting the dough in her hands until the mung bean was completely enveloped. The edges of the dough reminded me of the hem of a ballerina's tutu.

The rice balls were lined up, ready for their dip in the sweet and gingery syrup, a cozy and comforting mouthful. I was warmed by the heat from the stove and the heat from the pot. Her hands, confident and adept with her tools, moved to an inner rhythm. She was relaxed doing what she loved.

"Will you teach me Má, one day?" I asked, still lying on the floor.

She nodded, flour floating around her like fairy dust. A smile came to her face. The skin around her eyes crinkled.

"Help me clean up," she said.

I smiled too and stood up, the blanket abandoned on the floor, as I no longer needed its safety, and bounced over to her.

My childhood memories were sprinkled with these quiet moments with Má, warmth from her nearness as the heat from the cooking fires enveloped me and warded off the chill of the outside world. In these moments, when she set down her burdens and focussed on what she loved doing, I saw glimpses of Má's light as a soft glow of orange from a single candle to help illuminate my way.

It wasn't always like that.

There were moments when Má's light was a raging fire threatening all in its path, burning so hot it could blister the skin.

One evening when I was a teenager, we had just finished dinner, the three of us. I must have been in junior high as we lived in the two-storey rental house on Beverley Street with the green exterior. Porcelain bowls. Plastic chopsticks. Large ceramic plates. Medium ceramic plates. All the plates were mismatched and chipped. There was one dark brown plate that was the size of my palm that had a curved lip, perhaps donated to us or bought at a garage sale. It was the ugliest thing we owned but we used it at every meal.

Jen and I were sitting on the couch watching TV just a few feet away from the table.

The dishes were still on the table.

I heard ceramic breaking on the table. I stood up and looked back.

"Không!" Má shouted.

She broke another dish on the table, the ugly brown one. Her hands moved faster than normal. She continued in Vietnamese. "I was waiting for you to clean up. A test."

Má slammed two porcelain rice bowls on the table, breaking one in three pieces while the other one rolled off the table onto the threadbare grey carpet, rice and soya sauce spilling. "You never clean up!"

Jen and I just stood there.

"You two don't do anything! I do everything!" Má shouted in Vietnamese.

Had Jen and I sat for too long? Why hadn't we cleaned up? Were we waiting for instruction? Did we really not do anything ever?

Má went into her bedroom, only a few steps away, and slammed the door.

Jen picked up the shards with her bare hands and wrapped them in old newspapers. She didn't say anything; her lips were a thin line. Leftover rice and meat stuck to some of the pieces. She wiped the table with an old cloth. There were fresh chips in the faux-marble laminate tabletop. I stood there. I remember confusion and then emptiness.

The next evening, we all sat at the same table, Má and Jen speaking as if nothing had happened. I stared at the new chips in the table to remind myself I hadn't just imagined the whole incident, and made sure to clear the dishes after we ate. I missed that ugly brown plate.

It was not the first outburst or the last. There were times Má's words cut deep. There were times I cried, times I stared into space unsure of what to think, times I felt empty inside. There were times I disappointed Má and times Má disappointed me.

As a child, I could not see beyond my own hurt and anger. Why did Má do these things? Didn't she know I burrowed in my bed, tears staining my pillow, not wanting to leave my room? Didn't she know I sometimes flinched unlocking the front door, not sure which version of Má I would find inside? When my belly was twisted in knots and my hands clenched at my sides, I wondered, if Ba had been around, would it be different and how different would it be? Má would not have had to bear her weight alone. It cost her, but Jen and I paid the price too.

As an adult, I know Má did the best she could. To be a single mother in a foreign land, to rely on the charity of her deceased husband's family, to have her own mother and sisters so far away, her hands ached with the work that needed to be done. There were none of the community resources or support groups about mental wellness and parenting practices that are available now. Lying in bed at night, Má must have rubbed her hands together worrying whether Jen and I would grow up to be proper Vietnamese women. What would people think of her and how she'd raised us? I imagined her yearning for my father, running her hands along his face and down his body. To be hugged once again and to be the one who was cared for, to set down her weight so that he would pick it up, was something she would never have again. As she felt the pressures of the world squeezing in on her, and she blew up at me, the fire that consumed her burned me as well.

Má tried to teach intentional lessons about cooking and sewing; most of those lessons I never learned. Má tried to teach intentional lessons about working hard and being humble; some of those lessons I learned. And there were also unintentional lessons about being imperfect, being frustrated and out of control, being so lonely the abyss threatened to swallow you up. All of those lessons I learned.

As a grandmother retiree, Má goes swimming with her group of friends almost daily. She enjoys the feel of her hands pushing against the cool water. It is an indulgence she now allows herself. She cooks rice noodle soup and fried tofu for Lexi and Evan, hoping to serve up nourishment. At night, my mom rubs her hands together worrying whether my daughter and my son will become "proper" adults.

The mudra for my mother would be the varada mudra—gesture of compassion.

My Sister's Hands

The mudra for my sister would be the karana mudra—gesture with which demons are expelled. The palm faces out and up, the middle two fingers point down to touch the thumb while the index and pinkie fingers extend up.

I was always mesmerized watching her hands. Nimble and soft, her fingers curved backwards when she pointed them up. She could push her thumb way back, double-jointed she called it.

I always watched her hands when she danced. The flick of her wrist and the circular motions mesmerized me, the way she led with the pinkie, moving down and out with all the fingers trailing behind and around, like a bird swooping down and rising back to heaven. In one of the folk dances she danced in Folklorama for the Saigon Pavilion, she and the other five female dancers lined up one behind the other in one straight column. They all wore shiny emerald green áo dàis. Jen, being the tallest dancer, was at the front of the column. She swooped her arms above her head, and placed her wrists together, with the backs of her hands touching, and fingers curved and pointing away. The second person in line raised her arms as if creating a Y with her arms, palms positioned upward, in contrast to Jen's hand position. The third dancer raised her arms slightly below, palms down. The fourth dancer held her arms completely perpendicular to the ground, palms up. The fifth and sixth dancers held their hands lower and closer to their bodies, palms up and down respectively. Looking straight on, the audience would see only one woman, Jen, with twelve arms, outstretched, intentional, assured. And when the music started playing again, the hands would start to move. They moved through each of the positions, until at the sixth position at the bottom, when the dancer made a fluid swooping motion back to the first position above the head, wrists touching.

As a child, I was dazzled by the effect of the multi-handed lady, the multiple hands moving as one entity. As an adult, I appreciate it as an homage to Quan Âm, whether conscious or excavated from the choreographer's Buddhist upbringing. The many hands to share the work, the many hands to save and bring comfort to as many people as possible.

I wondered if my sister needed so many hands to be able to handle everything that came her way. Perhaps she needed more hands to shield herself both from the realities of the world and to defend those she loved. After all of that, did she have enough hands to take care of herself?

She was ten when we came to Canada. She'd had a full life in Vietnam, close friends in the neighbourhood, her books, regular visits with cousins and aunties and uncles and grandparents. Má and Ba were only parts of her whole. Her life shrank when we landed in Canada, unfamiliar as we were with the language and the strange food. It was a hard thing to start over in a new country, trying to figure out things for herself while her parents were also starting over and stumbling.

And then her world shrank even more when Ba died. Her life changed more than mine did. She was fourteen and I was only seven. My good fortune of having fuzzy childhood memories of that dark time after his passing contrasted with her bad luck of having vivid recollections and the realization that everything would be different. Ba had brought her to this country and he had abandoned her. Ba left her to hold in her hands everything that needed to be done, from calling the cable company, to attending my parent-teacher interviews, to dealing with Má's high expectations. Burdened by new responsibilities, she had to grow up overnight.

I will always remember the day Jen took me downtown on the bus to Eaton's and sacrificed her lunch money to let me buy the purple outfit for Barbie I so desperately wanted. She was always doing things like that for me. When Jen went to the movies with her friends, she took me along. When she went to work at Gourmet Cup, she took me along and I sat in the corner and read until it was closing time and I helped mop the floors.

Her hands were constantly moving, especially when speaking. She reminded me of a conductor of an orchestra or a Wiccan building a spell. She wove a guardian spell around me, sheltering me from the things I should not see, both inside and outside the house.

There were moments when she couldn't shield me, when she didn't have enough hands. When I was in university, Má had another outburst. We lived on Simcoe Street then, in a house with two tiny bedrooms, so Má slept on a fold-out couch every night. There was hardly room to breathe; we were always in each others' way, three adult women in a cramped space. I don't remember the event that preceded the outburst. I just remember Má screaming, ranting, babbling almost incoherently. Then Jen left. She left through the front door and she didn't slam it shut, like in the movies, but she didn't close it all the way and the cold winter chill flooded in. I had to close it and lock the door behind her. Then I hid in my room.

Jen left me. For her to leave me, she must have had to go so badly. It may have been worse for all of us if she had tried to take me with her. It would have taken too long to gather up all our things or answer any of my questions. We were grown-ups, yet always children during these outbursts.

Jen came home that night. All was quiet. Má was already in bed on her fold-out couch. When my sister opened the front door, I believe Má pretended to be asleep only a few steps away. I pretended to be asleep in my twin bed only a few feet away. They never spoke about it. I never spoke about it with Jen.

My sister moves away from the past, shielding herself. There is not a moment to stop, to reflect, to reconcile with the past. Unlike me, she moves towards the future, not turning back. She is not defined by the past nor held captive by it. She twirls and spins, hops and dances away from its bindings, to avoid being trapped.

Her life reflects this constant movement away from the past. As a lawyer, Jen uses her hands to work for the rights and claims of her clients, guiding them through laws and regulations. She is her own boss and works long hours. She volunteers for various organizations. She drives Má to go grocery shopping and takes her to her doctor's appointments. She and I run together, training for races and relays.

As a proud auntie, she has woven the same guardian spell around Lexi and Evan that she wove around me. For three years, she acted as Lexi's dance mom, living out her own dreams with Lexi. She held Lexi's hand crossing the parking lot on the way to practice. She helped Lexi slip on her ballet flats, tied the strings tight and tucked them into her shoes. My sister sat and watched her niece through the glass every Saturday morning. Jen was with Lexi for every extension, every hop and turn. During the performances, she ran through the moves in her mind as Lexi danced on stage.

She is for my kids what she was for me, my shield against the world. She is their Má Hai, their second mother.

Jen helped me with my homework, talked me through tricky situations with friends and co-workers, and taught me a million other lessons about how to be a person in the world. I also learned unintentional lessons from Jen. To guard others, I must guard myself from harm. To protect others, I must protect myself first. What comes to mind is the safety video before a flight takes off: secure your own oxygen mask before securing the oxygen mask for another person.

The mudra for my sister would be the karana mudra—gesture of protection.

My Daughter's Hands

The mudra for my daughter would be the vajra mudra—gesture of knowledge. One hand makes a fist with the palm facing out and up, the index finger extended upwards, while the other fingers enclose the thumb. The other hand, palm inward, envelopes the extended index finger of the first hand.

I can still fit my hand over Lexi's hand, completely engulf hers with mine. Her hand often grasped my index finger when she was a baby. She will still hold my hand when I reach for it, her small palm fitting into my own palm, to swing our arms. At some point, she will no longer want to hold hands in public with her mama.

Her hands are small, her fingers thin and bony. There is usually dirt underneath the fingernails, likely Play-Doh, soil, or grass from the schoolyard.

As a toddler, she constantly clutched a treasured object in one fist and only let it go to grab another precious item—perhaps an upgrade in her mind. It could have been anything, a plastic ball, a breadstick, a bit of string. The ultimate prize was mama's smart phone. I chased after her to retrieve it as she toddled away from me. When I took it from her tight grasp, she wailed and slammed her body on the floor, her heart broken and her face wet with tears. She operated on both intuition and impulse, figuring out her own mind and emotions, discovering boundaries, learning new relationships, and making new connections. It must have been comforting for her to hold onto something.

Lexi still needed comforting when she was six years old and she was testing to advance from her taekwondo yellow belt to blue stripe belt. She was probably one of the youngest to test for this belt level. The dojang was an open space with high ceilings and blue mats Velcro-ed together covering the floor. The scent of a locker room was strong; sweat, bodies, and deodorant all mixed together. Dozens of kids sat on the mats, stretching, while their parents sat on benches around the testing floor.

"I don't want to do this, Mama," she said to me before the test, huddling close. She looked around at the other kids testing. Seeing a familiar face would have lessened her anxiety.

I crouched down and took her hands, fitting them into mine. "Lexi, you're ready. You're so brave and you're so strong. Your teachers wouldn't ask you to test if you weren't ready."

The quivering of her lower lip. The fear in her eyes. She retracted her hands and began to move them up to her face to play with her lips between her fingers, her nervous tick.

I had a flash of memory, envisioning the tiny infant in my arms, skeptical, then the toddler, curious. Now she was a serious girl, watching.

"Let's warm up together," I said.

We sat down away from the other testers. Ryan was busy trying to keep three-year-old Evan occupied, following him around the practice area.

"I see other yellow belts testing. It's not just you, ok?"

"I don't know anyone," she said.

She drew strength from her relationships with others.

When it was time, I kissed her and sent her to sit with the other testers. It was out of my hands now.

All of the kids testing for blue-stripe belts performed together, demonstrating a series of punches, kicks, and patterns that were required to pass this level. As Lexi punched and kicked, she seemed distracted, watching others. She was not focussed on her own movements as she completed pattern number one and pattern number two, along with the other kids. Master P. noticed as well. Master P. asked to check Lexi's pattern. This meant she had to perform pattern number two a second time, this time, in front of the instructors, the other students, and the parents – all by herself.

I sucked in a breath. What would she do? Would she freeze? Refuse? Stop, cry, and run away? What would I have done at six years old? At six, I wouldn't have made it past white belt.

Lexi began the first couple of moves, as if from muscle memory, a low punch to the left, forward punch, pivot to the right, forward punch, and then she paused.

It seemed like the pause stretched to eternity. I thought—this was it; she will wilt and crumble, it'll all fall apart, and we will take her home, defeated.

She kept moving. She was not rushed at all. She was steady and deliberate. Every move was thought-through and crisp, full and complete lines. She did not cheat herself nor her instructors. Then she finished.

I realized the pause gave her time to gather strength in her fists. She'd needed the pause to generate energy from inside and hold that energy coiled within her fingers, like a spring. She needed to focus inward, undistracted by the people around her. She had told me testing for this belt was important to her, so I should have known she would not fail. She seemed to embody her father in that moment. She would not break. She was a tree with a solid stance.

She is steady, Alexis Ánh, Ánh meaning ray of light in Vietnamese; she roared into the world ten days earlier than expected, rushing to be born. So impatient she couldn't wait any longer, the doctor needed to cut me and pull her out; she'd been in distress, in high dramatic fashion. Má hadn't even made it to the delivery room, Lexi seemed that eager to be born. Her eyes were open immediately from birth, not wanting to miss anything. Deep pools of darkness—too big for her face then and too big for her face now. The nurse laid her on my chest minutes after birth, her hot breath on my skin, her hands in tight fists. On her first day of life, she scratched her face when her mittens fell off, her fingers long and lean.

She had been tethered to me as a baby, on my travels with Inanna through the underworld. Now as a fully separate entity walking her own path in life, she strikes me as completely familiar and yet changing all the time. Now she is full of questions.

"Where's your dad, Mama?" It seemed out of the blue one day at bedtime. I had never told her before. Strange how I had never thought to tell her. Má wouldn't have told her either as she told me very little when I was growing up. Lexi knew Má as Bà Ngoại, and Ryan's parents as Grandma and Grandpa, but where was my Ba, her Ông Ngoại?

"He passed away, honey. You know the altar at Bà Ngoại and Hai's house? You see his picture?"

"So he's dead?"

"Yes he is. And he is still with us. That's what I believe."

"I believe that too."

Lexi at age seven is the same age I was when I lost my father, when my life shifted. It's a strange thought—the circle of life, the parallels, but also the differences between me and my daughter, between my reality and hers. I look in my child's eyes to see myself, expecting to see the nervous quiet girl I was. Instead I find, reflected through her eyes, confidence and a lightness of spirit I don't know if I ever possessed.

I believe Lexi knows more about the world than I did at her age; she has certainly seen more and has experienced more. We have taken her travelling around Canada, the U.S., Mexico, Cuba, and Vietnam. Her favourite foods are crunchy noodles and tacos and sushi. She has played soccer every spring since she was four years old. She is athletic, an accomplished reader, and always curious about people, observing closely, asking questions and checking understanding.

And in other ways, she does not know much; her life has been stable. She has only known a solid foundation, living in one house, raised by two parents, her biggest concern possibly being the next toy or book she wants. She is healthy. She has never known hunger, abandonment, or a shattering loss. There has been very little heartache in her life. For this I feel incredibly blessed. I would not wish on her the struggles I went through immigrating to Canada and the challenges of my childhood. I would not wish on her my struggles with my identity. I want to protect her from the terrors of the world.

Yet I also do not want her to be so sheltered that she is ill equipped for life. I want to build her resiliency. She will one day know life is not just about birthday parties and happy sunny days, new clothes and fast food. She will one day know too much. I want her to have the tools in her invisible back-pack to pull out as she needs them. One day, the weight of knowledge will motivate her and mobilize her. I want her to not turn away from what is hard and scary, instead, to grow up to discover her gifts and use those gifts in service of others, to some purpose. This is my wish for her.

I wish that legacy to form the foundation of the lessons I will attempt to impart as I deliver into her hands books about myths and legends from around the world, books about past injustices and inequalities, and books about empathy and empowerment. I play with her fingers before bedtime as we talk about gender identity, feminism, privilege, God and spirit, everything and anything. There will also be unintentional lessons she will glean from me, the times she is watching me when I don't notice, in my interactions with her and her brother when I feel the fire burning inside me as it burned hot in Má.

Lexi is revealing herself to be a great teacher through her questions and her curiosity. In attempting to ensure Lexi learns what is valuable, I am also making sure I learn those lessons, too.

The mudra for my daughter would be vajra mudra—gesture of understanding.

My Hands

It used to be that the mudra for me would be the dhyana mudra—gesture of absolute balance, meditation. Both hands rested on my lap with the palms up, one on top of the other, the fingers fully stretched out, and the thumbs meeting to form a triangle between the overlapping palms.

If I had needed my hands to type on the laptop, they typed. If I needed them to wash dishes, they washed. When required, they fulfilled their duties, but no more than that. When I did not need them, they rested. When I sat still, my hands rested on my lap with my palms facing up. My hands only moved when needed.

My life reflected this stability for a time. I had been content to move in a predictable direction with a predictable speed. Other than my toddler years in Vietnam and a couple of years in Toronto, I'd called Winnipeg home all my life. Ryan and I celebrated our 10-year wedding anniversary with a vacation without the kids. I received my 15-year long service award at work.

I thought I had a clear direction for the rest of my life, a path to follow that was supposed to bring me success and happiness. Since my hands were open when they rested, I was open to receiving more in my life, my hands inviting more. I had been waiting for something to fall into my hands. I had been waiting for spirit to come to me, the inactive object that was acted upon.

The mudra for me had been the dhyana mudra—gesture of absolute balance, meditation.

No longer.

As I engage my mind in active meditation to create the mental mandala and create energy within myself, I find myself channelling that energy through my actions. A body in motion will remain in uniform motion unless acted upon by a force. If I am the active force in my own life, can I disrupt the speed and the direction of my life? I break through the inertia and change my path.

My mudra changes as I change. The new gesture for me would be both of my arms bent ninety degrees at the elbows, palms facing down, and both hands move.

I rocked both my babies to sleep before putting them down in their cribs. Lexi, in particular, craved motion. I swaddled her tightly, as if in a straightjacket, both arms glued to her sides. I held her with my arms bent, her head folded inward toward my breast. My one arm cradled her head, neck, and back and my other arm supported her butt and knees. She wailed ooo-la oooo-la oooo-la in her angry cracking voice, while her eyes stared at me accusingly. She was so tired and yet did not know how to fall asleep without my help. I did the bounce-and-sway, I did mini-squats walking along the hallway, and I swung her back and forth in my arms. I moved all the different ways I could think of, up and down and side to side. I walked the length of the main floor, doing a circuit around the ottoman in the family room, around the island in the kitchen, through the dining room to the study in the front, and through the hallway back to the family room around the ottoman again. Sometimes I did the circuit in the darkness from spatial memory at three a.m. I held Lexi tightly, my arms bent at the elbows.

I hold my arms bent ninety degrees at the elbows when I run. I took up running to reclaim some time outside of my role as mother and wife and worker. I devoted many evenings and early mornings to running as I trained for my first half-marathon. A half-marathon is thirteen miles, or twenty-one kilometres, that is probably many thousands of steps. And the kilometres I ran training for the half-marathon, must equal hundreds of thousands of steps. I theorized in distance, I ran a bunch of times around the perimeter of Winnipeg, or the coastline of Vietnam, or one-five-hundredth of the distance from the earth to the moon. I actually had no idea about distances, but I knew I covered a lot of ground. As I ran around my neighbourhood countless times, usually taking the same route, looping around the same trees and parks and houses, running in circles again and again, I always appreciated the total distance I'd travelled. I appreciated how far I had come, and also coming back to where I started.

When I run, I swing my arms, a natural sway, a rhythm to keep the pace, focusing on the next step and the next step. My hands are usually in loose fists by my side, my fingers curling in. Starting off in an easy jog, I set the exhale and the inhale, and adjust clothing or music or water bottle. After warming up, I pick up my pace, lengthen my strides and shorten my breaths. I tense up my hands, straighten my fingers, and pump my arms hard, like I am slicing the air, pushing aside all the mind clutter, and hacking away at my worries and stressors. If I'm on a straight pedestrian path with no one else around, I even close my eyes for a few moments. Feel the wind rush past my cheeks and hear my blood rushing between my ears, not sensing my legs beneath me. I visualize moving toward a goal, the glittery light of achievement in front of me, the actual distance representing the milestones of my inner journey.

At work, I sit or stand at my workstation, and stare at dual monitors. I bend my arms at the elbows, place my wrists on the gel pad, and move my fingers over the keys, in repetitive motion. Thoughts turn into sentences and paragraphs, emails and reports and proposals. Or I move my entire right hand, shifting the mouse around the screens. I never learned to type with my fingers on certain keys in their resting position. Since I've been typing for over twenty years, I can type without looking at the keyboard, or looking only very briefly. My fingers remember the location of the letters and numbers and symbols.

At home, I sit at my desk in the study, surrounded by talismans and rocks collected through my travels. I type on my purple laptop, with my elbows bent, and fingers flying across the keyboard. Sometimes very slowly and purposefully. Sometimes in a flurry of activity.

> Not fast enough. Capture.
> Too many thoughts.
> A mind sandstorm.
> A picture to capture.
> Words now. Fill in later.
> Don't lose the flow.
> Grasp it before it's gone.

I use my smartphone and laptop almost exclusively when writing. I write by hand, pen on paper, only when I am brainstorming or journaling.

Focus and intention. I translate bursts of thought and strings of ideas through my fingers, shaping them into letters and words on the screen. A blank screen, a white page, that is then filled with black letters, the cursor moving word by word and line by line thrills me. Theory becomes action.

As the word count moves from tens of words to hundreds to thousands, I harness creation via my hands into my words. My imagination and my own life spill forth onto paper and screen. No longer just in my mind, it's in the world now, word by word. I am no longer waiting. I am doing.

I think of Má's hands, wrinkled and tired yet still useful. Jen's hands are graceful and strong. Lexi's hands are busy, reaching. All of their hands, at one time or another, in one way or another, held me up, pulled me up, revealed lessons I am grateful to have learned. Doing our best with what we have. Being gentle with others and therefore with myself. These lessons have all helped teach me to be the heroine in my own story, to create momentum to move beyond my circumstances to create the life I want.

I look at my hands hovering above the keyboard. On my right hand, a white scar of an old accident between my index finger and thumb, runs to the other side of my palm. Veins tinted blue underneath suggest the first signs of wrinkles. I splay them out – as if magic will burst from my fingertips in sparks and flames – and then relax them. Now as my hands move across the keyboard, I move beyond the Dark Days, beyond grief, and most importantly, beyond inertia, to fulfill my dreams.

Writing is my active meditation, like creating mandalas. I find something powerful and enchanting in creating something from nothing. It brings me closer to spirit, to the universe, and to my true self. A tingling in my finger and in my hands. A deep hum in my body. These sensations tell me I am doing what I am meant to do. Creating is a powerful endeavour and has a powerful effect. Typing over and over, repeating the cycles of writing and rewriting, I continue circling to get to the centre.

As I move, as I become more active, something happens. The bits and pieces of myself begin to shift and reach toward each other, rearranging themselves in a different order, building on the strong foundation of ancestor worship. Also, I become aware of more pieces of myself, pieces that have always been there, but hidden, within pockets of darkness inside me. My moving hands conjure a storm of light, all the colours in a prism, illuminating these pieces of myself.

There is no need to search for threads. I am not in need. I am not in need of anything outside myself. As I begin to understand this, I know that there is more I need to do. As my hands transform the space around me, I know I must also use my voice.

The sacred gesture for me would be the gesture of creation. Both arms are bent at the elbows. Palms facing down. One or both hands move. Energy flows from my mind through my fingers and into the world, rippling through the universe.

The gesture is not Buddhist in form. The gesture is entirely mine.

I change my movements to change my life.

Nine: Sacred Speech

I CONTINUE MY EXPLORATION of the practices of Buddhism. The practice of mandala helps me sharpen my focus on the present moment. And tap into my creativity. The practice of mudra helps me channel my creative energy through my hands. I also channel this energy through my voice, reciting mantras. As I move from passive believer to active seeker, I'm most unsure of moving into the realm of mantra. It is the realm that is the most unfamiliar to me.

Mantra, in Sanskrit, means the thought behind speech or action. In Buddhism, a mantra is a mystical syllable, a word or phrase or sound repeated in a meditative way. As the universe is made up of sounds, vibrations, and frequencies, reciting mantras is a way to connect a seeker with these universal sounds. I focus on the practice of mantra with the hope of finding a close connection to spirit.

Mantras had been present throughout my upbringing, yet I did not find meaning in them. When Ba passed away, we knelt on the carpet at the Buddhist temple in Toronto, wrapped in white robes, white being the colour of grief, while monks clad in saffron robes chanted. Two years after Bà Ngoại passed away, at the end of the mourning period, we knelt on the reed mats at her house in Trảng Bàng, where Má had grown up. I wore a white headband. A monk was chanting. When Bà Nội passed away, at the ceremony one hundred days after she left the land of the living, we sat on the cool stone floor in her house in Trảng Bàng where Ba had grown up. I wore a white headband. A bald monk chanted.

Rhythmic and hypnotic, these sacred sounds carried from this life to the afterlife. The vibrations and the soothing sounds washed over us mourners.

I always wondered if the chanting was for those who had passed on to the next world or for those left behind in this world. The mourners pushed the syllables into the air, short, short, long, short, long, long, high notes and low, again and again. I imagined the vibrations dissolving the veil between the living and the dead, for the briefest of moments, to soothe the heart and connect to spirit.

I didn't chant along.

In my childhood home, on Ba's altar, Má set up an audio player, a black box that fit into my palm and only had an on/off button and volume control. I recall a silver lotus stamped on the back. The sole purpose of the device was to play in a continuous loop. The low hum of a monk's voice chanted, in Vietnamese I believed, though it could have been Sanskrit. His voice was like water trickling along the curves of a stream, carried along by the forces of nature and the universe, until it found its ending was its beginning and began again.

Má had the audio player on all the time, continuous white noise during dinner time, study time, trickling through my dreams at night. I always wondered, but never asked, what was the intention of the chanting. If the chanting was supposed to be for Ba, his family had automated the process. Perhaps the chanting was for us, to give us strength and hope, encouragement to keep going every day.

I didn't chant along.

At Chùa Hải Hội, on the night of the Lunar New Year, one of the rare occasions on which we visited the temple, we knelt on the floor beneath the statues of Golden Buddhas and prayer books were passed around. The printing in these books was of low-quality, the edges of each letter fuzzy; there were endless tissue-paper thin pages of mono-syllabic words. To my adolescent self, they were incomprehensible, more like magical spells, although like everyone else in the room, I could have pronounced the words phonetically. Dozens and dozens of voices chanted along, consolidating and intensifying the message. I didn't know what would be conjured by such spells.

I didn't chant along.

Just as I didn't light incense when Má cúnged to the ancestors at home as a child. Just as I didn't wear any talismans of faith as a child. I wanted to be a believer, but had too many un-asked, so un-answered, questions. I didn't want to be a fake and participate in the rituals and ceremonies when I knew I had not found faith.

As I move along my journey as an adult, I am more open to using my voice. I am open to breaking the silence and the stillness. Sound is a disturbance in the air, a change in pressure and density as it moves through space. The energy deep within my diaphragm pushes outward in sound wave vibrations, sound brought forth into existence. From high school physics I recall that the shape of sound waves are longitudinal, and the more tightly spaced the waves, the higher the frequency of the sounds. I visualize the sounds that I create travelling through the universe and reflecting as echoes, or refracting as either focussed or dispersed waves, or attenuating the further the waves travel.

I think of the waves as thought manifested into the universe through sound. In doing so, I give the thought power. I give the thought life, breathe life into it, so it may continue to take root in the real world, grow and flourish. It is the manifestation of intentional focus. I no longer seek threads as binding material. I no longer focus on the substances outside myself.

Om Mani Padme Hum

The phrase Om Mani Padme Hum is from Sanskrit.

The translation: the jewel is in the lotus.

If I only learn one Buddhist mantra, this is the one to know. It is the heart of Buddhist teachings, thought to be the fundamental mantra. My understanding is that by chanting the mantra, we are teaching or reminding ourselves to understand one thing—wisdom (the jewel) is in ourselves (the lotus). The sacred gem of wisdom lies within the lotus petals of our hearts and each facet of the gem shines outward from within. This mantra is intended to calm the mind and transcend thought.

Om Mani Padme Hum is related to Avalokitesvara, bodhisattva of mercy. The same bodhisattva, who in Vietnam, transformed into Quan Âm. All my roads lead back to Quan Âm it seemed. In Canada or Vietnam. However, after calling out to her after my miscarriage, I no longer chased the Goddess of Mercy. I loosened my desperation to get to know her. I no longer wait for her. I have stepped back, allowing her image to soften and move off to the side, no longer in the centre of my mind. Blurry around the edges, she now exists in the background.

Má still wears Quan Âm's image, golden and shimmering, around her neck. Quan Âm's shadow still falls over my life. I still think of the goddess fondly, as a gentle presence, and she will be a part of my life always. But I no longer think of her as my saviour.

When I attempt to say this mantra aloud, at my desk at home, the words do not come out. I stand in my bathroom and say it softly, even though no one else is there. I sit cross-legged in the family room, in sunlit space and warm air. I try a few times when I am alone in the house, with no one around to hear me, but it feels strange. The words feel forced, a bubble in my mouth, hollow and without weight. I might have the cognitive under-standing, yet I have no connection to the words. It's a challenge to relate to the words as sounds, without meaning. I attempt to focus on the sounds themselves but begin to criticize myself. My pitch is too high. I'm not as loud as I should be. I am not breathing from deep within and I cannot sus-tain the phrase, I need to break my pacing too often. I almost feel silly, an actress playing a part, a novice casting a spell meant for a great sorceress. It does not feel authentic to me and that surprises me. Am I truly open to this experience? What obstacles am I placing in my own way? These barriers are not there for mandala and mudra.

What do you think? What are your views? How do you feel? These ques-tions were not asked of me growing up. I was not encouraged or taught to give voice to my thoughts and opinions. Má did not invite questions. I could not voice my questions to Má about ancestor worship and cúng. I don't know if curiosity was something not encouraged in Vietnamese culture, if speaking up was discouraged. All I know is what was not encouraged in my house.

This left me wondering if my voice was valuable to anyone. I was unsure if anyone would listen, if anyone would care. If I said something, and no one cared, did it even happen? *If a tree falls in a forest and no one is around to hear it, did it make a sound?* Would the words I vocalized still create a dis-turbance in the air, waves passing through particles? Yet if no one heard me, if my words did not reach the ears of another human being, were they real? I could hear the sound of my own voice, but I did not know if that mattered.

As an adult now, speaking aloud still does not come easily to me. I need to work at it. The fact that I am having difficulty with this Buddhist mantra reveals to me the power that speech holds. When I was a stranger to myself, lost in the wilderness during the Dark Days of work reductions, I spoke unkindly and brought negativity into the world. This behaviour also revealed to me the power that speech can hold. To say something aloud and bring it forth in the universe is a powerful act.

I acknowledge my boundaries. This mantra is not mine.

Om

Om is the sacred sound of the universe in the language of Sanskrit. My understanding is that saying Om aloud will bring harmony to my body. Chanting it will help me with the fundamental vibration of all things. Om is the natural vibration of the universe, the sound of all things. It may be chanted at the beginning or at the ending of an endeavour such as before or after a meal, a meditation session, or a prayer. Whatever my intention, Om is said to help me to focus on it. Perhaps this mantra could be more accessible to me.

Om is pronounced like the sound in "home" and not in "prom." There are three parts to the sound—A-U-M.

I drop my jaw and make an ahhh sound, as if opening my mouth for my doctor to check my throat. I extend the exhalation on the first part. I adjust my lips a little closer to make the uhhh sound, feeling resonance in my head and in my face, along my cheeks. When I feel I'm close to squeezing all the air out of my lungs, I close my lips and make the mmmm sound, feeling the hum in throat and in my chest.

Ahh ... uhhh ... mmmm.

Silence.

Ahh ... uhhh ... mmmm.

Silence.

Ahh ... uhhh ... mmmm.

I feel the vibrations move inside me, up through my chest and lungs, and out through the top of my head, fading away, each wave rippling away from my body. This practice feels like a cleanse, an adjustment, a realignment. The silence in-between the Oms is the pause between that which has passed and that which is to come. The silence is just as important as the sound itself, as it is a time of reflection and it is also a time of potential, like new snow, the breaking dawn of a new day.

Saying Om aloud is easier than saying Om Mani Padme Hum aloud. Yet engaging in both mantras is significantly more difficult for me than drawing mandala or performing mudra. I question whether this is the right path for me. I do not want to turn away from something because it is hard or because it will take work to master. Yet I must ponder the reasons why vocalizing is so difficult for me.

I was a quiet child, not used to hearing my own voice. At General Wolfe Junior High School, the gang tags on the shiny black front doors had to be painted over every few months; kids brought knives to school, and kids came to class and then dropped out, never to be heard from again.

As for me, my pink shirts from the bargain store matched my pink-rimmed glasses. I wore a mask of indifference even as I fretted over every social interaction, pulling the edges of my long-sleeved shirts over my knuckles to calm my nerves. Never one of the cool kids, I just didn't want to stand out.

In Language Arts class, we each had to stand in front of the class and read aloud our review of the book we had been reading. It was about a boy in a concentration camp during World War II. Standing there, feeling all eyes on me, sweat formed in my white training bra. My glasses were heavy on the bridge of my nose. Wanting more than anything to sit back down, I read my piece as quickly as I could, never looking up, my eyes dancing over my words written in cursive blue BIC pen faster than my mouth could move. I was not able to catch my breath fast enough, the words tumbling out one on top of another. After this torturous process, my classmates commented that my voice seemed shaky and they thought I was crying.

My reluctance to express myself, to raise my voice, was hard to overcome. I was not naturally chatty. I usually had to think to speak. I thought a lot but spoke very little. Writing in my diary and in my journal was how and where I felt safe to express myself. Speaking aloud was not a safe space. I could not imagine that I had something to say that was important and valuable enough to break the silence.

By saying Om, I am pushing myself to make unfamiliar sounds. I am calling power to myself, not with my mind or with my hands, but with my own true voice, and that is unsettling to me. Mandala and mudra feel authentic. I incorporate these practices into my life, noticing the linkages and weaving the practices into patterns already around me. Mandala and mudra are already relatable to my life. I see my loved ones in mandala and mudra. Yet Om remains completely in the realm of the unfamiliar. Again I feel like I am playing a role and it does not resonate with me.

This mantra is not mine.

My Own Mantras

As mandala and mudra have moved beyond the realm of institutional religion, so too has mantra. Mantra indicates a word or a phrase that is repeated, whether silently or aloud. The word or phrase is something fundamental to an individual. What values do you live by? What motivates you? What words calm you and centre you? The answers may form an individual's personal mantra.

My understanding is that a mantra may also help individuals practice mindfulness—to be in the present moment and to shift negative thinking to positive thinking. It is a way to bring the wandering mind back to the present and to interrupt the meandering thoughts before they stray too far. Using these parameters, phrases have formed in my mind and fallen from my lips when I have needed them. The mantras I have fashioned for myself have helped me find strength when the storm rages in other areas of my life.

Throughout my journey of motherhood, there have been moments when I wanted to check out. *That's it. I'm done.* These were moments when I was so sleep-deprived, I was seeing stars behind the actual objects I was looking at. I felt so unsure, so much a failure, all I wanted to do was crawl into bed and have no one bother me. I had to curl my fists together to hold in the frustration and annoyance.

I would put my baby down in the crib for the night, just to settle on the couch to pump breast milk into the flanges, careful not to waste a single drop as the let-down began. I still needed to wash all the bottles and pumping parts, sterilize all the bottles and parts and fold the laundry that had been sitting next to me for days. How did other moms get through it? I needed words of strength to get me through those days and nights.

Other days, already lunchtime, I would retreat to the bathroom to put in my contacts and brush my teeth, still in my pyjamas. I just needed five minutes of peace, to breathe and be still. I heard "Mama, Mama, Mama," on the other side and saw chubby fingers creeping under the door. I needed words of patience.

Or times when Lexi needed to go potty, but she couldn't pull down her leggings fast enough without my help, and I was still feeding Evan his bottle. I ripped the bottle out of Evan's mouth to rush to Lexi. Evan cried as he spilled his milk and Lexi cried as she peed down her leg. I needed words of comfort too.

I closed my eyes and muttered softly.

I repeated to myself:

Dig deep.
Dig deep.
Dig deep.

During the Dark Days at work, I dreamed of drafting my resignation letter. I didn't believe it was a fair deal—my mental wellness in exchange for a bi-weekly deposit to my bank account. Then things changed – the New Workplace emerged from the ashes of the Old Workplace.

After Evan was born, I was out of the workforce for a year. Coming back to work after maternity leave, returning to a job I had outgrown, I shouldn't have been surprised that the terrain had once again changed in my absence. Overgrown weeds, ideas and practices needed to be dug out. I was amazed to discover new seeds planted for a new variety of vegetation, ready to be nurtured. It was no longer the first New Workplace after the Old Workplace had passed on; now it was the second New Workplace;

more new colleagues, another new boss, and another new organizational structure. Another time of transition, shifting sands, and uncertainty in my role. I had been here before.

With the new seeds, I was able to tend to and harvest a new possibility for a different position in the second New Workplace. I was content. For a while. Then it shifted again. I was unhappy with this second new situation and my second New Leader. I had been here before. Through the original Dark Days and emerging from the wilderness as a new kind of employee a few years before, I already knew I would not give my heart away again.

I gazed at my reflection in the workplace washroom mirror and whispered aloud.

I repeated to myself:

Things are bad. They will change. Things are good. They will change. Things are bad. They will change. Things are good. They will change. Things are bad. They will change. Things are good. They will change.

"Are you a writer?"

At two separate book readings held years apart, authors posed that question to me after I asked them about their creative process, book structure, or the state of Canadian literature.

Each time my mind went blank. Sweat started to form on my upper lip.

"I am an aspiring writer," I said to the whole crowd. "I want to be a writer," I admitted out loud.

"You are a writer. Call yourself a writer," both authors said.

Who was I to call myself a writer? Even with the permission given by "real" published authors, I still couldn't do it. I could not give voice to that dream. Even though writing has always been a part of me. As a kid, I scribbled stories and fairy tales in my coil-bound notebook. I had a need inside me to put words together, characters together, worlds together.

My heroines, however, had pale skin and light-coloured hair, lived on the farm and ate meat and potatoes. These were the stories I knew; these were the stories I thought I should be writing. I was influenced by *Anne of Green Gables, Little House on the Prairie*, the fantastical worlds of Narnia and Middle Earth. With the exception of *Sadako and the Thousand Paper Cranes,* I don't recall reading about any characters of Asian descent, stories of the Asian experience. Growing up, I did not read about characters who looked like me and did not see my reality reflected in books.

In grade five, I wrote a story, "Above The Clouds" about a girl who was transported to the realm of the Greek gods and met Arachne. She was turned into a spider by the Goddess Athena for daring to boast that her weaving skills were greater. In grade six, I wrote about two girls who were best friends before one died of leukemia. In grade ten, for geography class, instead of a report, I wrote a short story, "A Day in the Life of Juan Diaz" about the climate in Cuba. In grade twelve, I wrote a short story, "The Earem Theorem" to explore my skepticism of the nature of truth regarding chemistry and physics.

I later discovered books by writers who existed at the margins, who had carved out space in-between. Authors reached out from their pages and spoke to my heart: I see you and I hear you and I am you. So many possibilities opened up when I identified with these writers. Power came from believing that writing could be in my future, power in seeing myself reflected in books. It was a blessing to hold deep inside when the world was a strange place, when I felt outside the realities of others, when I was the stranger, the only one, The Other. I will be forever grateful to those writers who revealed to me that my perspective was valuable and my experience worth telling. In university, after completing all my business-school homework, I stayed up very late and wrote a short story about a girl named Mai whose deceased mother returned to her in the form of a silver-scaled dragon who could freeze time with her icy breath.

After university, I discovered creative non-fiction—writing about true events in a literary way. To be a writer, I had thought you had to write poetry or fiction, and fiction was western, mystery, fantasy, or science fiction. Memoir, what was that? Not just autobiographies written by celebrities. More possibilities opened up. Creative non-fiction gave me permission to write my own tale, not dressed up in anything but my own tears, laughter and lived experiences. I didn't have to create a character that was me but not me. I could be my own character in my own story.

After Evan was born, I again went through writing starts and stops. I submitted bits and pieces of creative non-fiction essays here and there, usually as contest entries. But while I was trying to find a balance between juggling full-time work with two kids, writing moved to the background again. I didn't know if this was common.

About the time Lexi was five and Evan was two, I looked over the edge of the rest of my life. I was grateful for what I had in my life. It was a full life. An immigrant parent's dream. Did Ba peer from beyond the land of the living, proud that I had "made it"? Yet something was missing. I felt like I was skipping along the surface of my own life.

Disconnected.

A mother. A wife. A daughter. A career holder.

But where was I in all of it? I felt I had space to breathe again with the kids no longer in diapers or needing my constant attention. I gave myself permission to become the heroine of my own life again.

"What now?" I asked. Did I want to focus on my day career, to work my way up the corporate ladder? Did I want to learn how to become a better cook? Did I want to concentrate on my running, to train for more half-marathons after running my first? Not really.

Deep within, I knew what called to my spirit.

With everything else going on in my life, would it take me ten years to write a full-length book? Would anyone actually read it? Did that even matter? Who was I writing for, if not for myself? I couldn't stop writing if I tried.

Was writing my true path in life? I felt as if I was stealing moments— writing in a coffee shop after dropping Lexi off at a birthday party or visiting the public library during lunch breaks to do research, or thinking about a tricky transition in the shower. I limited myself to late night writing and editing when the kids were in bed, only after lunches were made, and the house was tidy (enough). Even when my brain hurt staring at the blinking cursor, I survived on peppermint tea and Doritos, before getting up to go to work the next day. I was snatching time whenever I could.

Could I commit to making writing a priority? As a dream, as a fantasy, it had been a glittery possibility, a mirage always in the distance. To make it a goal was to risk failure, risk disappointment, exposure and letting people read my soul.

To do the hard work, day after day.

To challenge myself to do this thing I said I had always loved.

To take a risk and call myself a writer.

I repeat to myself:

> *I am a writer.*
> *I am a writer.*
> *I am a writer.*

* * *

When I published my first essay, I cried by myself when I got the acceptance email, utter joy that I achieved a dream of the heart. I told Ryan and the kids and we jumped up and down together as a family. We raised our voices to the sky and the vibrations rippled out to the universe. For the next few days, the glow, the thrill every time I told someone produced the same delicious feeling as when I was first pregnant with Lexi.

A few months after that, I had a second piece published in *Prairie Fire* magazine—their 40th anniversary edition. I was blessed to be invited to read an excerpt at the launch party.

I practised in the bathroom days before the reading. In the same bathroom where I couldn't vocalize Om well, I read my own words aloud, and pictured reading my own words to a live audience. My heart fluttered in my chest even though I was no longer that shaky-voiced girl in grade seven in front of her Language Arts class. I would speak at this event knowing I had something valuable to say, knowing that my voice mattered.

I sat in the second row, my fingers tingling, and waited for my turn. Writers were invited in alphabetical order so I was the last person to read. I smoothed the hem of my dress and adjusted its neckline. It had again been difficult to find the right garment for the occasion as I wanted to convey professionalism yet a sense of warmth. But after walking with Inanna and weaving together a garment, this knee-length A-line cut dress draped with crimson blossoms and fuchsia buds were the threads I needed.

I stood at the podium. The microphone tilted toward me like a ball of stardust tumbling from outer space, complete with comet tail. Time was suspended, but only for a moment. In those few milliseconds, I saw the crowd focussed on me, all eyes on me. I took a deep breath and pushed all the air out, planting my feet on the ground and straightening my back. It had been ingrained in me to step aside, to give way to the voices of others, so this was a terrifying moment.

I did not shrink. I did not waver. I had worked hard for this. I gave myself permission to have this space and time for myself.

I opened my mouth. Energy created within me carried to the outside world; thought materialized as sound. My own voice broke the silence, the words sounded clear, and my tone steady. I tried to regulate my breathing.

"I'll be reading the last section of my creative non-fiction piece 'Incense and Ancestors.' In the piece, I talk about the Vietnamese custom of ancestor worship. I also talk about the Trưng sisters, who are historical and mythological figures, freedom fighters, from ancient Vietnam."

I looked down at my copy of *Prairie Fire* magazine in my hands and found my words in print. These words flowed easily and naturally as the Buddhist mantras never did. The soundwaves danced over the particles in the air, vibrating and resonating within the eardrums of the people in the audience. The waves I created began to reflect and refract around the room, moving into spaces that were not visible, stretching and reaching further than I imagined possible. Saying my words aloud, my words became my mantra, and changed me from the inside out. I wasn't alone in the forest. I spoke and people heard me.

Creating vibrations that resonate throughout the universe is a source of power. This was my offering. I felt the hum deep within and the tingling in my fingertips, the sensations I always felt when I was close to spirit. Before I finished my reading, I looked out to the audience, to write the memory in my mind. I would recall and savour it in future moments when I was unsure and lonely in my writing. It was the first time I read aloud my published work.

I ended off:
"A crack in the window, a doorway not quite shut, a lid slightly ajar.
Enough of an opening through which

light may pass,

air may flow,

water may seep,

and spirit may come. "

My mentor, sitting in the front row, came up and embraced me. Although it had been years since we had worked together, we had met up from time to time, at the restaurant, recreating our rituals, and talking about writing. My extended family took pictures of me posed at the writing table and asked me for my autograph. Má and Jen were there, beaming, proud—it meant the world to me to share this moment with them. I was writing myself into my own story.

At age thirty-six, I had earned my first paid publication, a powerful and meaningful personal achievement. Because I felt it took me so long to get here, I appreciate the journey that much more.

I claim my voice.

I am a writer.
I am a writer.
I am a writer.

* * *

I integrate writing into my life now. If I hold on too tight—too much writing—I neglect my health or am not present with Lexi and Evan or take Ryan for granted. If my grip is too loose—too little writing and I miss it—I am cranky with my kids and do not feel like me, losing myself to all my other roles, not honouring myself. I strive every day to achieve the right balance. I fail. I keep trying.

I've learned I can only deny my truth for so long. The truth leaks out. It bubbles up. It breaks through when it can no longer be denied. I am forever grateful to—and inspired by—authors who lead the way, who hold space for writers from marginalized communities, so I have a path to walk. I'm closer to becoming the person I want to be. I now embrace the writer in me and pursue my true life's journey.

When I write, I focus on the next word and the next word and the next. I also focus on the flashes of ideas or sparks of thought that spin out of me, and try to capture them. I feel both inside myself and outside myself. I feel both grounded to the earth and floating in the sky.

I embrace the same spark when spirit enters my space and brushes up against me. I travelled to sacred spaces that called out to me and compelled me to ask the questions about my origin story, about being a heroine in my own life, and what to believe about the afterlife. A light flickered within me after I walked with Inanna through the underworld. I wandered the wilderness after the Dark Days to find the promised land. I embraced the sparks of spirit during these experiences.

When I read my work aloud, sometimes I cry, sometimes I laugh, and sometimes I cringe. Something deep within me resonates with the outside world, resonates with the universe itself. Creation – creating something from nothing. Being a writer gets me closer to spirit. I am active in the typing, in the pondering, in the imaginings in this practice of active meditation. Mantra opens the way for me, just like mandala and mudra. I push and pull on the forces of the universe, within the laws of physics, the laws of spirit, and choose my own path, my destiny.

"What are you?" This is a question I always get asked regarding my identity. It is related to race, culture, nationality, gender identity, etc. And spiritual affiliation.

I am still trying to figure out my spiritual beliefs after deciding that I am spiritual but not religious. I know what I am not. I am not a Buddhist. I am not a follower of the Goddess. I do not subscribe to any one institutional religion. The challenge is how to set the foundation for mindfulness and meditation and spirituality outside institutional religion.

I am a seeker. My true life's journey is in the seeking.

The challenge for me is to integrate the mundane daily life of work and writing (where I spend so much of my time) with the extraordinary moments of spiritual clarity (these are rare and cherished moments that may be relived and reflected on, nourishing my spirit to live in the ordinary moments). I work to integrate the two kinds of experiences, and to merge the spiritual moments in the mundane moments. I work to make the mundane spiritual.

What do I believe? What is my foundation?

I choose to believe I have the power to influence my immediate environment and that influence could have far reaching effects on the earth. That is an immense power.

I choose to believe when someone passes away from this life, this reality, they are never truly gone. They remain with us in energy form, and once in a while, for whatever reason, we sense them, closer to our existence. This could be linked to the time of year, the phase of the moon, or the mind state of the seeker. No energy is lost and no energy is created, it reincarnates and cycles through the universe. Stardust and light of supernovas eons past find their way to us.

I choose to believe there are laws of the universe. Spiritual laws. Spirit is not an entity, not a personified being but manifests as different figures in different space-times as bridges to that which cannot be known. Spirit is unknowable, a flash in the mind, a spark, a scent, a tingling. Humans have created more tangibles for the five senses: houses of worship, idols depicting what the goddesses and gods may look like, symbols, talismans and physical objects. We create rituals and ceremonies, write prayers, designate holy spaces and sacred lands. The push and pull of spirit, chasing it and creating it and listening for it and receiving it.

Mythology informs my world view at its most fundamental levels—creation, life after death, heroines and heroes, animals, explanation of natural forces and the environment, warning stories, love, tricksters and transformers. I see myself and the people around me in those myths. Ancestor worship forms my roots, the launching point for my spiritual search.

My way in is through my foundation of Buddhism for spiritual practice. I contemplate mandala, perform mudra, and voice mantra. These are the three touchstones of mind, body, and speech. These practices bring me closer to the spirit within myself. For each of the three elements, I shift away from the traditional Buddhist form. I discover my own ways to spirit, to connect to myself and to the universe.

Mudra and mandala are about other people and my connection to others. Mantra is all about me and my voice. What I bring to the universe.

My mantras are my own.

My writing is my own.

My spirituality is my own.

I wouldn't just leave my job, leave my family, leave my life to seek out the meaning of spirit travelling the world, travelling outside my immediate surroundings and outside my reality. I have responsibilities and commitments and people I love deeply; it is not all about me. So to change my life, to manifest my destiny, to create my own future, I need to do so within the life I already have. I must create the extraordinary in my ordinary life. Day by day, tiny little change by tiny little change, to change my life, to align it to my destiny, I must work at it.

As I practise active meditation, as I begin to move within myself to change the space around me, to change the universe itself, what was foggy becomes clearer. The bits and pieces of myself that have been hidden, emerge into the light, and shift and weave together. I did not find anything in my travels around the world that I didn't already have. I have all the threads and binding material I need within me. I'm realizing that I already have the answers to the questions I ponder. When I travelled to the underworld with Inanna, that was not the end of my journey. The journey doesn't end. I emerge from the wilderness to discover that the promised land is where I already am.

While I see nothingness in space, space is truly not empty; instead, it is filled with interstellar gas and dust. The dust of the stars gave life to me and to all life in the universe. The starlight burns brilliantly in the darkness. I am not empty either, I am not nothingness. I am boundless and all the universe exists within me. I am my own light.

Night after night, sitting cross-legged at my desk, peppermint tea ready, I write. Me and my purple laptop and the next word and the next word.

I read my words aloud to myself, "Growing up, it was my job to clean Ba's altar every month, sweeping away dust, sweeping away grey ashes from the incense holder, sweeping away last month's prayers and wishes."

In writing about my journey, reaching the end, I come back to the beginning.

I create my own spirituality. I have all the light inside me. Divinity within. Light and the universe in me. Spirit is in the practice, not in the belief.

I see the interconnection between self and the universe. What I seek externally has been within me all along, within the spaces in between everything. I am working in that space – active writing and active spiritual practice.

I am the centre. Starting at myself and ending with myself.

Bibliography

Chapter 1

Trưng sisters committing suicide
Corfield, Justin. *The History of Vietnam*. Greenwood Press, 2008.

The last battle
Vo, Nghia M. and Nguyen Ngoc Bich. *The Trung Sisters Revisited*. Nghia M. Vo, 2015.

Chapter 2

Saqqara and Delphi
Ingpen, Robert and Philip Wilkinson. *Encyclopedia of Mysterious Places: The life and legends of ancient sites around the world*. Dragon's World Ltd., 1990.

Xi'an
Lin, Zhang. *The Qin Dynasty Terra-Cotta Arm of Dreams*. Xi'an Press, 2005.

Glastonbury
Lloyd, Polly. *About Glastonbury*. Bossiney Books Ltd., second edition 1999.

Hạ Long Bay
Martin, Paul. *Land of the Ascending Dragon: Rediscovering Vietnam*. Gates and Bridges, 1997.

Hồ Hoàn Kiếm
Tran, Thi Minh Phuoc. *Vietnamese Children's Favorite Stories*. Tuttle Publishing, 2015.

Chapter 3

Inanna poem
Campbell, Joseph. *The Hero with a Thousand Faces.* New World Library, third edition, 2008.

Story of Inanna
Storm, Rachel. *The Encyclopedia of Eastern Mythology.* Anness Publishing Limited, 1999.

Chapter 4, 5, 6

Bridges, William. *Getting Them Through the Wilderness.* 2006, https://wmbridges.com/resources/transition-management-articles/getting-them-through-wilderness/

Chapter 4

Quan Âm and the legend connected to the One Pillar Pagoda
Logan, William S. *Hanoi: Biography of a City.* University of New South Wales Press Ltd., 2000.

Chapter 5

Quan Âm and the legend of Miao Shan
Campbell, June. *Traveller in Space: In Search of Female Identity in Tibetan Buddhism.* The Athlone Press, 1996.

Chapter 6

Quan Âm and the legend of Thị Kính
Monaghan, Patricia. *Encyclopedia of Goddesses and Heroines.* New World Library, 2014.

Chapter 7

Symbols of the mandala
Lowenstein, Tom. *The Vision of the Buddha*. Duncan Baird Publishers, 1996.

Description of all the elements of the mandala
Storm, Rachel. *The Encyclopedia of Eastern Mythology*. Anness Publishing Limited, 1999.

Chapter 8

The names and descriptions of the mudras
Jansen, Eva Rudy. *The Book of Buddhas: Ritual Symbolism used on Buddhist Statuary and Ritual Objects*. Binkey Kok Publications, 1990.

Chapter 9

Three Mysteries – body, mind, speech
Lowenstein, Tom. *The Vision of the Buddha*. Duncan Baird Publishers, 1996.

Om mantra and Om Mani Padme Hum mantra
Kaivayl, Alanna. *Sacred Sound: Discovering the Myth and Meaning of Mantra & Kirtan*. New World Library, 2014.

Acknowledgements

Deepest gratitude to all who have supported me and believed in this book.

Many thanks to Michael Mirolla and everyone at Guernica Editions. Cover designer Rafael Chimicatti was flexible and so patient. When I asked for a more bluey purple and a font that looked more accessible, he got what I was trying to say and offered new looks. Editor Julie Roorda was responsive and thoughtful. She asked insightful questions and always supported me in my vision for the book.

The beginning chapters of the book were sparks of memory and myth captured in essays while working with Katherine Bitney through the Manitoba Writers' Guild mentorship. We sat across from each many times sharing cake. I'm forever grateful for her wisdom, kindness, and faith.

I wrote the initial draft of the book doing my mentorship with May Q. Wong through Diaspora Dialogues. Thanks to President Helen Walsh and Program Manager Zalika Reid-Benta for giving me the opportunity to participate in this mentorship program. May was perceptive and pulled from me not only what I wanted to write about, but what I needed to write about. I learned to trust my voice and write for myself.

Working with Joan Dixon for developmental edits helped me define and refine the shape of the manuscript. She taught me what to look for in editing and how to rework, yet again, when I thought I was done.

With the support of Diaspora Dialogues, I worked with Chelene Knight on editing, polishing, and finalizing the manuscript. From her, I learned how to weave form and structure with substance.

I'm so grateful to these women who played a part in helping me complete my book baby.

At one time, I thought writing about spirituality and faith was a lonely endeavour. Who else had these big questions that I had? I'm so blessed to find myself in community with amazing writers Pam Couture, Lana Cullis, Jannie Edwards, Meharoona Ghani, Kitty Hoffman, Sheniz Janmohamed, Tamara Jong, Vickie MacArthur and many others. Hugs to Lori

Sebastianutti for our nourishing chats about faith-based work and the writing life.

Susan Scott has been an incredible mentor, a deity at the crossroads, who mapped the terrain of spiritual life writing for so many of us, and who guides me still. I'm so honoured she has written the Foreword.

Earlier versions of some of the chapters have been previously published. *Gates and Goddesses* was previously published in *The Fiddlehead*, edited by Rowan McCandless. *Incense and Ancestors* was previously published in *Prairie Fire Magazine*, edited by Janine Tschuncky and Lindsey Childs. *Sacred Hands* was previously published in *the same Literary Journal* and *Raising Her Voice Anthology*, edited by Rachel Holbrook. Deepest gratitude to these literary magazines who gave my pieces a home and gave me the confidence to keep writing.

Many thanks to all the authors who took the time to read my work and offer an endorsement: Hollay Ghadery, Sally Ito, Rowan McCandless, Mai Nguyen, Susan Olding, Shanon Sinn, Betsy Warland, and Lindsay Wong.

This book is about me, and it's about so many of the closest people to me—my friends, my cousins and extended family, my grandparents, my sister, my mom, my kids, my husband, and my ancestors. I wouldn't have the strength to write about it all without their support and love. I hold that love close as I continue my journey as a seeker.

About the Author

Linda Trinh is a Vietnamese Canadian author who writes nonfiction and fiction for adults and children. She explores identity, cultural background, and spirituality. Linda's creative nonfiction has appeared in literary magazines such as *The Fiddlehead, Room, Prairie Fire*, and *This* Magazine. Her short fiction has appeared in anthologies such as *Black Cat* anthology and *Alternate Plains: Stories of Prairie Speculative Fiction*. She has been nominated for two National Magazine Awards.

Her award-winning early chapter book series, *The Nguyen Kids*, explores Vietnamese culture and identity with elements of the supernatural, spirituality, and social justice woven in.

She has studied with published writers in writing programs and courses through such institutions as Humber College, Athabasca College, the University of British Columbia, the Manitoba Writers' Guild's mentoring program and through the mentorship program through Diaspora Dialogues.

She lives with her family in Winnipeg, on ancestral lands, Treaty 1 territory, traditional territory of the Anishinaabeg, Cree, Oji-Cree, Dakota, and Dene Peoples, and on the National Homeland of the Red River Métis.

Website: lindaytrinh.com

Printed by Imprimerie Gauvin
Gatineau, Québec